MCCALLIE

A Century of
Inspiring Boys and Building Men

by Barry Parker '63

PARKER HOOD
PRESS

This book is made possible in part

through the generous support of our

Sponsors

Steven K. Austin M.D., P.C.
Chattanooga, TN

Robert Betz Associates, Inc.
Arlington, VA

Fletcher Bright Company
Chattanooga, TN

The Caldwell Foundation, Inc.
Chattanooga, TN

Coca-Cola Bottling Company
Chattanooga, TN

The Law Offices of Lew Conner
Nashville, TN

The Dickson Foundation, Inc.
Charlotte, NC

Dolan, Pollak & Schram Development Company, LLC
New York, NY

Driscoll Group
Winston-Salem, NC

Foxbrush Farm
Cornersville, TN

Huffaker & Trimble
Chattanooga, TN

Hutcheson Ferry Farm
Whitesburg, GA

The Keith Corporation
Charlotte, NC

Lawson Electric Company, Inc.
Chattanooga, TN

LDS Consulting, Inc.
Scottsdale, AZ

Manier & Herod
Nashville, TN

The Michaels Family Charitable Foundation
Atlanta, GA

Miller & Martin PLLC
Chattanooga, TN/Atlanta, GA/
Nashville, TN

Olan Mills, Inc.
Chattanooga, TN

Morgan Stanley
Atlanta, GA

The Allen Morris Company
Coral Gables, FL

Morris, Manning & Martin, LLP
Atlanta, GA

moseley, inc.
Manassas, VA

Sponsors

Motes Advertising, Inc.
Chattanooga, TN

Nelson Energy, Inc.
Shreveport, LA

Nichols Fleet Equipment, Inc.
Chattanooga, TN

Pantheon Investments LLC
Chattanooga, TN

Prudential Carolinas Realty
Winston-Salem, NC

Raines Brothers, Inc.
Chattanooga, TN

T. S. Raulston, Inc.
Chattanooga, TN

River Street Architecture, LLC
Chattanooga, TN

**Thomas C. Ruff, Jr. & Associates,
   Attorneys at Law**
Charlotte, NC

Shaw Industries Group, Inc.
Dalton, GA

Starkey Printing Company
Chattanooga, TN

Stowers Machinery Corporation
Knoxville, TN

SunTrust Bank
Chattanooga, TN

TSWII
Chattanooga, TN

Turner Foundation, Inc.
Atlanta, GA

Veritas Properties, LC
Wickliffe, KY

Vintage Development Company
Charlotte, NC

The Walker Companies
Jackson, MS

**Shannon P. Warrenfells, Jr.,
   D.D.S.**
Durham, NC

**Wyman, Green & Blalock
   Real Estate, Inc.**
Bradenton, FL

Sports and Activity Center from McCallie Lake

McCALLIE:

A Century of Inspiring Boys and Building Men

Copyright © 2005 by The McCallie School
Text copyright © 2005 by Barry Parker
Photography copyright © 2005 by Robin Hood

For information, contact: Office of Public Affairs, McCallie
School, 500 Dodds Avenue, Chattanooga, TN 37404;
telephone: 423/493-5615; e-mail: info@mccallie.org.

Published by Parker Hood Press, Inc., 100 Cherokee
Boulevard, Suite 2006, Chattanooga, TN 37405; phone:
423/267-6294; e-mail: parkerhoodpress@yahoo.com

Grateful acknowledgment for photographs is made to the
following: pp. iv and viii; Bob Krist; pp. 1, 2, 4 and 33,
Chattanooga Regional History Museum.

Designed by Robertson Design, Inc., Brentwood, TN
Separations by iocolor, Seattle, WA
Printed in China through C&C Offset Printing Co., Inc.

ISBN: 0-9645704-6-7

FIRST EDITION

Contents

McCallie

A Century of
Inspiring Boys and Building Men

Dedication

This book is gratefully dedicated to the faculty and staff
who inspired ten decades of McCallie men in the classroom
and on the field — conveying knowledge, instilling values
and changing lives.

Acknowledgments

I wish to thank those members of the McCallie School family —
faculty, staff, alumni and friends — who graciously contributed time and
effort to make this book possible. In particular, a large measure of
gratitude is due George Hazard '64, author of *When We Came to the Ridge*.
His meticulous, loving research of McCallie's early history and the trove of
taped interviews he created were invaluable in bringing this work to life.

Grateful appreciation goes to Dr. Kirk Walker for his keen
involvement and thoughtful guidance throughout the project and to the
school's administrative staff, including Curtis Baggett, Rebecca Nelson
Edwards, Billy Faires, Anne Pitts, Mitzi Smith and May Wood, all of
whom displayed enthusiasm for the undertaking despite the many
requests that attended it. My special thanks to Casey Rowland for
assembling the intricate listings for the Appendix and to Bill Steverson,
who helped bring us aboard the project.

I also thank those who graciously welcomed me in person and by
phone to talk about the school that shaped their lives, including: Curtis
Baggett '65, Steve Bartlett, Lewellyn Boyd '46, Arthur Lee Burns, Jr. '55,
Fletcher Bright '49, Herb Cohn '49, Eleanor McCallie Cooper, Mel
Cooper, Hal Daughdrill '73, Whitney Durand '60, Rob Huffaker '78, Dr.
David McCallie '40, Spencer McCallie III '55, T. Hooke McCallie '30, Dr.
Charles Sienknecht '33, Frank Thompson '33 (deceased), Dr. Kirk Walker
'69, Whitlow Wallace '63 and Harry Weill '32.

—Barry Parker

Chapter One

Laying the Foundation

IN THE SPRING OF 1905, Chattanooga was flexing its industrial and entrepreneurial muscle. The southern riverbanks of a city that would proclaim itself the "Dynamo of Dixie" bristled with blast furnaces and smokestacks. Business ventures flourished. A Scotsman had established an insurance company that would rise to national prominence. For one dollar, two local attorneys had pestered an Atlanta pharmacist into selling them the national bottling rights to a beverage he had concocted and believed was destined to be a fountain drink only. And a publisher had built a gold-domed headquarters for his newspaper before leaving the city and traveling north to buy *The New York Times*. The creation of wealth was evident in handsome municipal buildings, in the brick retail stores that lined bustling Market and Broad streets and in the generous sprinkling of mansions in Riverview and Fort Wood and along the flanks of Cameron Hill.

Drawn by Chattanooga's vitality and promise, a population that would more than triple between 1880 and 1910 was stretching the boundaries of the city. The Walnut Street Bridge now spanned the Tennessee River, connecting the wooded hills of the north shore with downtown. To the east, a brick viaduct carried horse-drawn wagons and gas-powered cars over the spaghetti-like tangle of railroad-yard tracks that crossed McCallie Avenue. A cable car climbed to the cloudy top of Lookout Mountain, and an electric streetcar line pushed spokes of rail into the growing neighborhoods of Highland Park, St. Elmo and East Lake and up and over the 800-foot-high north-south barrier of Missionary Ridge.

No one could have watched the city's rise from the ashes of the Civil War with more appreciation than the Reverend Thomas Hooke McCallie. The 67-year-old, semi-retired Presbyterian minister had been the only clergyman to remain in Chattanooga throughout the bitter war from 1861 to 1865. Depending on who controlled the city at any time, Confederate or Union troops sat in the pews of his First Presbyterian Church at Market and Seventh streets as he preached on Sundays. He was convicted of treason at one point and, another time, threatened with confiscation of his home and land near town at the head of McCallie Avenue. His mother's entreaties saved the home, and pluck and good luck enabled him to escape sentencing and removal and survive a dozen other wartime entrapments.

In November 1863, he stood at the edge of his property and watched, awestruck, as Union soldiers charged Confederate placements on the crest of Missionary Ridge to the east. "The battle raged from Sherman Heights clean down to Rossville," he wrote in his memoir. "It was a terrible but a magnificent sight." The Southern troops were routed, and their retreat marked the beginning of the end for the Confederacy. The way was open for the Union Army's

Elegant homes that crowned the 125-foot-high bluff overlooking the Tennessee River near downtown Chattanooga at the start of the twentieth century reflected the city's growing wealth. The gold-domed building at the head of Eighth Street was built by future *New York Times* publisher Adolph Ochs.

assault on Atlanta and General Sherman's fiery march to the sea. Chattanooga and the rest of the South were about to enter the painful era of Reconstruction.

To this pivotal battlefield, the Reverend McCallie and his wife, Ellen, came in 1882. Fearing that his health was in permanent decline, he had retired his church pulpit, left the large, rambling homeplace in town and bought 80 acres for his family on the side of the ridge. They were officially in the country, two miles beyond the city limits. The land provided for little more than subsistence farming, supplying vegetables and berries, milk and cheese from a handful of cows and mutton from the sheep that grazed the steep hillsides. But as people fanned out from the growing city, the value of his land on the ridge and downtown kept climbing, and Reverend McCallie could sell parcels as financial needs arose.

Five decades after the Civil War, Chattanooga was a bustling manufacturing center. McCallie Avenue viaduct, at right, linked the commercial district, above, with Missionary Ridge on the outskirts of the city.

In 1891 he and Ellen, a small woman possessed of eyes like embers and "true grit," as her husband put it, built a three-story, 18-room brick and slate-roof castle of a home, with one corner shaped like a turret, to replace the smaller, two-story frame dwelling they had occupied on the Ridge. The McCallies needed the room. Here they would continue to raise 16 children, eight of whom would die before their 20th birthday, and here they would talk about the educational needs of the slowly reviving South.

The Rev. Thomas Hooke McCallie and his wife, Ellen Douglas, visit the Presbyterian campground at Montreat, NC in 1890. The couple lived in the frame McCallie homeplace on McCallie Avenue and Lindsay Street until 1882, when they moved to Missionary Ridge.

It is unknown when the subject of starting a private preparatory school for boys was first broached by the McCallies, but the family had a history of interest in education. The Reverend McCallie's ancestors came from Whithorne, a town near the southwest coast of Scotland within sight of the Irish Sea. As Calvinistic Presbyterians and students of the Bible, the McCallies valued literacy and learning. Twenty-one-year-old John McCallie emigrated to America in 1775, arriving in Philadelphia and finding his way to

Blount County in East Tennessee where the landscape resembled the green swells of the Scottish countryside he left behind.

His son, Thomas, who was the Reverend McCallie's father, set off from the Maryville area with 75 cents in his pocket to become a successful merchant and owner of bottom-land farms. He settled his family first in Rhea County, then, in the winter of 1841, moved them by flatboat to Chattanooga. He purchased 25 acres on a dirt road on high ground above the center of town and built a two-story frame house. This road that stretched from the Brainerd Mission to town became known as McCallie Avenue for the extensive McCallie homeplace anchoring one end of it. Called "Colonel Tom" for his service in the state militia, the successful merchant and farmer planted peach, apple and plum trees, worked a fine garden, kept a stable of horses and a number of cows and fattened hogs for meat that was cured in the smokehouse.

Thomas McCallie possessed a basic education but wanted more for his children and others in the blossoming community. His wife, Mary Hooke

Chattanooga was a pivotal battleground in the Civil War, occupied, in turn, by Southern and Northern troops. As the city slowly recovered from the ravages of war, the demand for college-preparatory schooling increased.

McCallie, had been a teacher, and with her blessing he built a brick school-house and recruited the first true educator to Chattanooga, Professor H.W. Alderhoff. Thus prepared by his parents for higher education, the Reverend McCallie was sent to Burritt College on the Cumberland Plateau in Spencer, TN. There he underwent a religious conversion, and later he made the decision to enter the ministry. His family supported his travel to New York City and three years of study at renowned Union Theological Seminary where he earned a doctor of divinity degree in 1859.

The Protestant work ethic, Scottish ruggedness and a strong Calvinistic faith were hallmarks of the McCallie family. A page of records from the family Bible begins with the marriage of Thomas "Colonel Tom" McCallie to Mary Hooke on December 26, 1831.

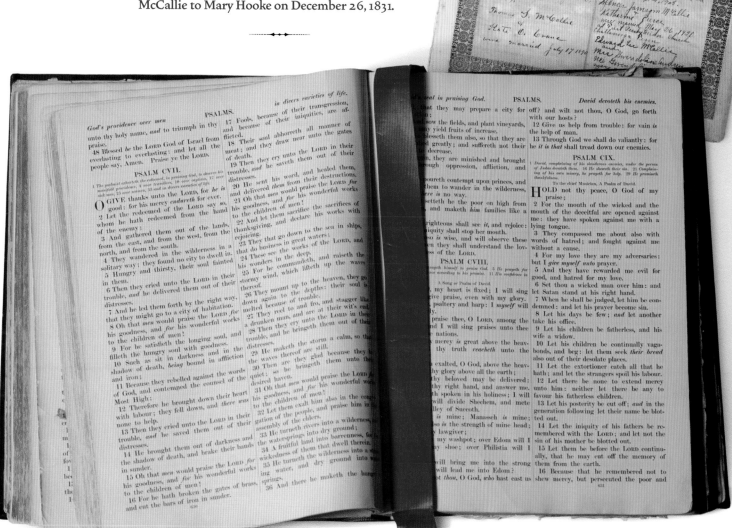

Shown with their parents are the five sons of Thomas Hooke and Ellen Douglas McCallie: from left, Douglas, Edward, Thomas (seated), Spencer and Park. The fanciful Victorian home on the side of Missionary Ridge where the boys were raised became the school's first dormitory.

As a Presbyterian minister and from first-hand experience, Reverend McCallie valued education, though he expected to preach its merits rather than deliver them personally. Yet when the Civil War ended and the ravaged city lacked basic services including schools, he consented to open one in his own home in September 1864. The decision was made easier by the need to support his family at a time when income from his ministry had dwindled to nothing. He enrolled between 60 and 80 children for one nine-month term, charging three-dollars per month for each pupil regardless of their grade. His cousin, Nellie Hooke, helped him teach. "I had always thought I would not like this occupation," he wrote, "but I threw myself into it heartily and enjoyed it..."

The Reverend McCallie's brief foray into teaching marked what could be called the first McCallie school. The experience operating a school was likely conveyed to his children and may have influenced some in their choice of education as a career. The oldest McCallie child to survive to adulthood, Grace, was born in March 1865 as her father's one-term school was ending. She became a teacher at Chattanooga High School and, later, a founder of Girls' Preparatory School in Chattanooga. The youngest of the McCallie children, Margaret Ellen, also became a teacher and chief assistant to Mary Gardner Bright, founder of the private Bright School for elementary students in Chattanooga.

Born between Grace and Ellen were six other surviving McCallie children: Julia, Thomas, Spencer, Park, Douglas and Edward. Julia married Sam Divine who managed the city's electric streetcar line. Douglas became a missionary in Korea, Tom became a revered minister as pastor of Chattanooga's Central Presbyterian Church, and Edward lived a colorful life as an adventurer. Spencer and Park plunged into the world of education with a special fervor. It would be their collaboration, with the support of their father and their family, that would set The McCallie School on its course.

I n the late spring of 1905, Spencer Jarnagin McCallie and James Park McCallie were living 83 miles apart and a thousand miles from the family's Missionary Ridge home. Twenty-five-year-old Park was in northern Indiana finishing a second year as mathematics instructor at Culver Military Academy. Before arriving at the attractive boys-school

Spencer McCallie, at right, was younger brother Park's best man when Park married his college sweetheart, Harriet "Hattie" Bibb of Charlottesville, VA, on March 24, 1904. At the time, the brothers appeared destined for careers in education far from Chattanooga.

campus on the shores of Lake Maxinkuckee, he had attended the University of Virginia where he displayed a rare blend of traits as a student of pure science and a devout Christian fundamentalist. A serious and dedicated scholar, in the course of seven straight years in Charlottesville, VA, he earned bachelor's and master's degrees and, in 1903, a doctorate degree in astronomy with additional work in mathematics and philosophy. His Ph.D. was one of only seven awarded in the field of astronomy by American universities that year.

In 1900, Spencer McCallie, shown here, was the 25-year-old superintendent of public schools in Cleveland, TN, a post he left after two years to enroll in the University of Chicago's master's program in education. Park, meanwhile, was awarded his doctoral degree in astronomy from the University of Virginia in June 1903.

Near the end of his first year of teaching at Culver, Park married his college sweetheart, Harriett Bibb of Charlottesville, on March 24, 1904. Their son, James Park, Jr. was born a year later. The young family moved into a new home on the Culver campus and settled into a life of domesticity: Hattie tending the home and the child; Park teaching his classes and gardening for recreation.

Park's older brother, Spencer, was another story. Half a head taller than his brother, twenty-nine-years of age and still single, Spencer, too, was a teacher, but his career path was as circuitous as Park's was straight. Spencer had attended Southwestern Presbyterian University in Clarksville, TN until he was expelled for a prank – some say for trying to tie a dead animal to a dean's door; others claim for spiking the punch of ministerial students at the school. The mischief was later forgiven, and he received both bachelor's and master's degrees from Southwestern. Meanwhile, he

In the fateful spring of 1905, Park was teaching his second year of mathematics at prestigious Culver Academy in Indiana while Spencer was preparing to leave Chicago for a teaching post at the University of Washington in Seattle.

taught science at Chattanooga High School and served for two years as the popular, young superintendent of public schools in nearby Cleveland, TN.

A man in perpetual motion, Spencer left the Cleveland post to enroll at the University of Chicago. In April 1905, while taking graduate courses at the university, he received an offer to teach at the University of Washington in Seattle. For a robust and adventurous man such as Spencer McCallie, a move to the pioneering Northwest would have been appealing.

With Spencer preparing to move to the far edge of the country; Ed graduating from Davidson College; the youngest McCallie sibling, 17-year-old Margaret Ellen, departing for Agnes Scott College, leaving an empty nest at home, and Park and Hattie raising a child in Northern Indiana, a critical moment had arrived for the McCallie family's dream of starting a school.

Despite his relative happiness and security at Culver, Park made a bold proposal. In letters written to Spencer and his father, Reverend McCallie, in May 1905, Park stated that if he and Spencer were ever to establish a "first class Univ(ersity) School," this fall was the time. To his father, whose property on the Ridge and financial backing were critical, Park stated: "I am anxious to come back to the old home and live in the South, and I believe this is the time now that will either sever us boys from the old home or weld us to it."

Spencer was less certain of the project and visited his brother at Culver the last weekend in May to discuss the idea at length. Park would later call their meeting "the turning point in our lives." The brothers addressed the daunting task of having just three months time to prepare a curriculum, a staff, a classroom building, and a campus for students enrolling in September. They talked about the need for such a school in their region and the competition that existed. There was already one preparatory school in Chattanooga, as Park and Spencer knew well: Park's alma mater, the Baylor University School.

———————

With the backing of six prominent Chattanoogans, 41-year-old John Roy Baylor, Jr. had been recruited to the city in the fall of 1893 to provide preparatory schooling for their sons and for other boys in the community who desired a college education. Chattanooga's public school system, established in 1872, offered a three-year high school curriculum that lacked the science and modern language courses required of entering college freshmen. A recent financial panic, meanwhile, had closed a number of private academies including the Caulkins School, which Spencer McCallie had attended, as well as the preparatory department of the city's Grant University. In September 1893, Chattanooga was without any of the private preparatory academies that were constantly surfacing and disappearing as itinerant, under-financed professors by the dozens came and went.

Professor Baylor opened his school in September by leasing the vacant McCallie homeplace on McCallie Avenue. Reverend McCallie, who had sons to send to the school, stipulated in the lease agreement that his boys be exempt from the school's hefty $100 tuition. Fourteen-year-old Park McCallie was one of 31 boys enrolled in the first class. "He (Prof. Baylor) was a burly man with a big voice," recalled Park, "and he had us properly cowed." But Park's academic talent earned Professor Baylor's interest and kindness. Park graduated in 1896 with the highest grade point average in the school's history to that time. Professor Baylor encouraged Park to enroll at Baylor's beloved alma mater, the University of Virginia, and helped gain Park a scholarship. The day Park left by train for Charlottesville, Baylor saw him off at Chattanooga's Central Station at 6:30 in the morning and handed his star pupil workbooks to go with a three-volume set of reference books he had already presented as a parting gift.

As both landlords and patrons of Baylor's academy, the McCallie family undoubtedly followed its fortunes. Though enrollment was stagnant, hovering at 50 students or less, the school's financial backers underwrote construction of a two-story brick building on Palmetto Street where the school moved in 1899. For a period of twelve years beginning in 1900, Professor Baylor opened the doors to girls to increase enrollment revenue, though they were never fully integrated in the curriculum and life of the predominantly boys' school.

What Park realized from his stay at Culver was how different a school could be from the academies that professors such as John Roy Baylor typically established in the South. Usually located in buildings in city neighborhoods where there were little or no grounds for recreation, these schools drilled students in Latin, Greek and modern languages, recitation, mathematics, English and basic science. As a classically trained educator, Professor Baylor opposed interscholastic athletics and granted no diplomas, believing the only credible test of a preparatory education was a student's performance on a college entrance exam.

Culver, on the other hand, was located in the countryside where it offered a spacious campus with a classroom building, library, chapel, athletic fields, a stadium, a gymnasium and a lake. Here, a boy could develop physically as well as academically. As a future campus, the McCallie farm on Missionary Ridge provided appealing natural features of its own: ample acreage for buildings and fields, a spring-fed, two-acre lake for recreation and a location that was easy to reach by streetcar yet a healthy distance from the congestion and temptations of town three miles away. Chattanooga had never seen the Culver model, and Park was eager to bring it home. "We wanted to give our lives to the South," he would later explain, "and felt that education in the South desperately needed every help it could get."

While Spencer's work had been in public education, not private, and his heart was inclined to Seattle, Park's enthusiasm for "a country day school for boys at the old family homestead" gave Spencer cause to consider. After the weekend discussion with Park at Culver, Spencer suggested they leave the decision to their family in Chattanooga. Spencer immediately wrote Reverend McCallie at the end of May 1905 asking that the parents and the two older siblings, Thomas and Grace, give their opinion. "If Park, with a wife and baby, has the grit to put his faith in the scheme," Spencer wrote his father, "I have not got the nerve to stand back and say, 'I am afraid.'" Spencer confessed he was "on the fence and ready to go either way; yet once in," he added, "I shall stick to Park and the school until he hollers 'quit.'"

Reverend McCallie's response on the family's behalf was a manifesto in the form of a letter he wrote and mailed to Park on June 1, 1905. He explained that he, Ellen, Grace and Thomas had met the evening before in his study above the oak staircase on the second floor of the Ridge home to debate the proposal. What emerged by consensus was a list of compelling reasons why the school should go forward immediately. The letter's opening statement reflected Reverend McCallie's view of any of life's work. "Our aim is not wealth," he wrote of the venture, "or even the having the family together, as desirable as this is, but the glory of God in Christ."

Then he made the concrete case for opening a school on Missionary Ridge that fall. First, the McCallies' two-story, frame house on the Ridge property was vacant and could be fitted for classes. The brick Victorian home where the parents currently lived, now empty of children, could be pressed into service as a dormitory, for it was quickly foreseen that the family's wide reputation in religious and educational circles might draw boarding students from a region that was short of preparatory schools.

Secondly, Chattanooga was growing rapidly, he wrote, and its prosperity had increased the number of local families who could afford private-school tuition. As for competition, Baylor School, in the family's view, "has not filled the whole opening here for the kind of a school you design" and Grant University,

A woman fishes in the spring-fed, two-acre lake that was part of the McCallie farm on Missionary Ridge and became the recreational centerpiece for the school campus.

which had dropped its preparatory program, "will scarcely stand in your way."

Furthermore, he declared that opening a school would test Spencer's and Park's mettle, and the struggle to keep it afloat would develop their character. It would also give them the opportunity to be their own boss, which was impossible at Culver or the University of Washington. "You would roll your own wheelbarrow," their father stated with feeling, "instead of drive some other man's cart."

Besides the availability of the two family houses and 40 acres of property for the school's use, Reverend McCallie offered to immediately furnish his sons between $2,000 and $2,500 in capital "to place you on your feet in the new enterprise." In return, he expected them to create "a Christian school and exercise a good, wholesome Christian influence on your pupils." Offering Christian training without a direct church affiliation would distinguish McCallie from other private schools. "The glory of God in Christ could be and should be your aim in your school," Reverend McCallie declared.

The four family members unanimously agree to "your commencing at once this fall," said the letter. Grace had an additional suggestion — that the

In 1904, the year before the school was founded, the McCallie farm clearing is visible (above) on the near slope of Missionary Ridge from a curve on Crest Road. Steel observation towers and granite monuments (left) dotted the top of the historic Ridge battlefield.

school accept girls as day students. Her opinion was based on the fact that a fourth-year certificate program at Chattanooga High drew girls only, demonstrating their desire for higher education. Reverend McCallie said he agreed with Grace's suggestion, but the family, he said, had not discussed the point. Park and Spencer were focused on an all-boys' school, however, and the issue of McCallie accepting girls received no further formal discussion. The next fall, Grace would join two fellow teachers from Chattanooga High, her cousin, Eula Jarnagin, and Tommie Duffy, in establishing Girls' Preparatory School.

Good to his word, Spencer accepted the family's decision and abandoned plans to move to Seattle. By mid-June, he had arrived in Chattanooga to begin promoting the new school and recruiting its first class of students. Two weeks later, Park, Hattie and their son, Parkie, left friends and their new house at Culver and returned to the Ridge. "My mother was a little fearful; definitely," said Anne McCallie of the move from Indiana. Park and Hattie McCallie were uprooting the family in hopes the idea for a school would succeed, and the brothers, Park and Spencer, had less than 100 days to see that it did.

------ ◆◆ ------

Spencer wasted not a moment in getting out the word. Within a week of his homecoming, the *Chattanooga News* and *Chattanooga Times* were trumpeting plans for the new school. The *News* reported that the school would not only prepare young men to "meet the entrance requirements of the leading colleges" but equip them for business life as well. In addition to the course work, each student would be required to participate in "gymnastics and games." For this purpose, baseball and football fields, tennis courts and a running track would be built at the bottom of the ridge. The school, said the article, was prepared to accept 16 boarding students and a larger number of day students. Classes would be taught by four to five college-educated instructors.

The *Times* ran a statement from Spencer praising the school's Missionary Ridge location as "unsurpassed for the object which we have in view – the development of a sound mind in a sound body." He said students would receive individualized instruction and their class work would be augmented by field trips. He also publicized the brothers' credentials. As an instructor at Culver, Park had gained first-hand knowledge of the best methods in secondary education, Spencer said. For his part, he had held teaching and school administrative posts and had recently studied the newest pedagogical theories at the University of Chicago. "We believe," Spencer declared, "our experience in school work will enable us to make our school first class in every respect."

To back up the talk, the brothers rolled up their sleeves. They transformed the nine-room former family residence into classrooms and offices and created dorm rooms in the 18-room family home. A 30- by 60-foot gymnasium was an unplanned expense and to pare the price to $1,800, Spencer and Park toiled in the August heat to lay the foundation themselves. Though so small that the baskets hung on walls padded to cushion the collision from lay-ups and players could sink shots from center court, the modest, peak-roofed structure was still the first gym in the area and underscored the McCallies' commitment to athletics. To round out the teaching staff of Spencer and Park, they enlisted the help of their 21-year-old brother, Ed, who convinced his Davidson College roommate, Len White, to follow him to the new school that fall. Both had played college football and would be important as coaches and players as well as instructors. Headmasters and teachers alike would earn $50 a month.

During the summer of 1905, Spencer and Park personally laid the foundation for the school's first constructed building, a tiny gym that stood between McCallie Lake and a streetcar trestle running up the Ridge. The gym served notice of the brothers' intention to stress physical as well as academic development when their school opened in the fall.

Chapter One

By August 1905, advertisements began appearing in local and regional newspapers for the school's fall term which would begin the third week in September. The ads touted the school's "high and healthful" location and spirited athletic program as well as academic preparation. While the ads were appearing, the brothers traveled in search of boarders: Spencer to Cleveland, Knoxville and Memphis, Park to Charlottesville, and Ed to the Davidson campus in North Carolina and to Rome, GA.

In 99 days, Spencer and Park had transformed a farm into a campus, and the response from local residents was encouraging. The McCallie family had deep roots and long associations in Chattanooga and East Tennessee, and parents seemed willing to trust their sons to the well-educated Spencer and Park. And giving the venture additional credibility was the backing of the respected Reverend McCallie, who the sons listed as school founder. Throughout August and early September, the brothers heard of intentions to send boys to their school when it opened on September 21. Yet, as the day rapidly approached, they had to wonder if promises made would be promises kept.

Chapter Two

Fertile Ground

1905-1920

ED McCALLIE leaned his broad shoulders from the window of the frame house that had recently been fitted with classrooms and gazed at the scene unfolding below. Rumbling uphill from the streetcar junction at Dodds Avenue and Chamberlain Street a few minutes after eight o' clock on a cool, late-September morning was the Missionary Ridge-line trolley. It climbed slowly toward Ed McCallie, the electric wire above it crackling, then swerved left onto Kyle Street. The motorman pulled the bell chord and applied the brakes. McCallie peered intently at the trolley. It was packed with teenage boys. One by one, they bounded from the car. As their numbers grew, McCallie yelled to anyone in earshot: "All of Chattanooga is coming to school."

The strong turnout for the first day of class, Thursday, September 21, 1905, was a vote of confidence in the McCallies and worthy of a shout. Sandy-haired Clay McFarland had been the first to register. Another 42 ninth through twelfth graders joined him that first day. Some were transfers from Chattanooga High; six had previously attended Baylor. Many lived in the nearby neighborhoods of Highland Park and East Lake. Two days later, five more boys would enroll, and ten more would join the student body later in the term. The hastily established school had drawn 58 boys, including eight boarding students, its first year, probably twice the number Spencer and Park had conservatively expected.

Students purchased school books from T.H. Payne & Company for courses in English, Latin, Greek, German, French, math, physics and history. Spencer, Park and

When McCallie opened in fall 1905, it offered a bucolic, 40-acre ridge-side campus in the country. The small house at the left had been converted to classrooms, and the family residence on the right, Founder's Home, served as a dormitory. The lake is at the bottom of the property. (Opposite) This hand bell was used to ring-in classes when the school's electrical system failed.

Len White carried the major teaching assignments. Ed McCallie, an All-American- caliber football player, concentrated on coaching. Reverend McCallie, who served as school chaplain, taught one Bible class and gave short morning devotionals, walking from his Founder's Home residence to the small frame school building just a few yards to the south of it. Hattie McCallie helped keep the business books, manage the kitchen and oversee meals for the boarders.

The momentum of the summer swept Spencer, now 30, and Park, 26, into their first school year as co-headmasters and the beginning of a fruitful 44-year collaboration. Spencer's powerful, magnetic personality would be put to use attracting teachers and students. A man of immense vitality, heartiness and personal charm, affectionately called "Fessor" by students, he was destined to be the school's "Mr. Outside." An exuberant storyteller and sought-after public speaker, he employed dramatic gestures and abundant humor whether speaking to seventh graders in his Bible class or businessmen at a Kiwanis luncheon. Park McCallie said you always knew where his brother, Spencer, sat at a gathering by the bursts of laughter at his end of the table.

If Spencer gave the McCallie venture its buoyancy, Park provided the

Between 1905 and 1920, when this faculty composite appeared in the *Pennant*, McCallie attracted gifted teachers. Among them were Clarence Wilcox (second row, second from left), who became headmaster at Darlington School and R. Fred Thomason (second row, far right), who was Registrar at the University of Tennessee for many years. Frances Thronton Strang (top row, second from left), the school's first female teacher, elevated the English program. The venture begun by Spencer (fourth row, far right) and Park (third row, far left) was meeting with early success.

(Opposite) More than 1,800 spectators watched McCallie and Baylor play to a scoreless tie on October 31, 1908 at the University of Chattanooga's Chamberlain Field. The rivalry quickly drew crowds too large for either school to host. Competition was an integral part of the McCallie experience, and the school fielded teams in every high school sport.

ballast. His meticulous and frugal nature would be an asset in handling the school's business affairs, and his rectitude and religious zeal would create some of its hallmark institutions. Where Spencer was gregarious and spontaneous, Park was cerebral, precise and reserved. Nothing, however, masked his passion for spreading the Gospel through any means possible. While short in physical stature, "Doctor" conveyed the commanding presence of a highly educated and devout individual, and men of power and wealth treated him with deference. Spencer McCallie would say that the biggest man he knew, after his father, was his brother, Park.

The brothers had correctly gauged the interest in sports by boys and their parents, and they made athletic competition a strong suit. In early September before school began, Ed McCallie and Len White were already holding football practice. Both had played college ball at Davidson. White had also played at South Carolina, and McCallie would continue his college football career by playing at Cornell the next year. The game of football was still in its infancy, and coaches were allowed to play with their teams, giving the McCallie squad a

Because the children of Rev. T.H. and Ellen McCallie had grown and moved from home, space became available in their rambling, three-story Victorian house for boarding students, helping make the school's founding possible. Over the years, children, grandchildren and great-grandchildren of the McCallies returned to the ancestral home as resident faculty members of the school.

distinct advantage. With Ed McCallie regularly playing halfback and Len White substituting at tackle, the 1905 team posted a 4-0-2 record, including the 41-0 trouncing of a loosely organized Baylor team.

McCallie's bucolic campus, spirited sports program and youthful headmasters and teaching staff gave the school an unmistakable vitality and caused an increasing number of families to take notice. So did the establishment of the Honor System. Park borrowed it from the University of Virginia, and the McCallie School Senate, under President Knox Smartt, voted to adopt the program beginning with first-term exams in January 1906. The code stipulated that anyone caught cheating on an exam would be tried by a tribunal of the

Senate, which would render a verdict and assign punishment. It also established a pledge, honoring a student's signed word that he had not given or received help on an in-class or take-home test. Lying and stealing were later added to cheating as punishable offenses under the Honor System.

The formal adoption of the code was an example of the McCallies' uncompromising attitude toward integrity. Other private schools talked about honor in student behavior but few adopted McCallie's stringent standards as immediately as McCallie. And for good reason; the Honor System was not easy to embrace. Students were required to report fellow students, which flew in the face of the boyhood code that denounced "squealing." In the early years of the System, one member of the Senate told his Senate colleagues he was doing the hardest thing he had ever done in his life – by turning in his brother for cheating. Punishment, too, could be emotionally painful. The apology to the entire student body that for years was demanded seemed akin to a public-square shaming. Yet the System immediately took root, gained widespread acceptance and respect, and became a pillar of the McCallie experience. Many students claimed its value lasted a lifetime.

By early 1906, the school's financial underpinning required addressing. On a snowy evening in January, Park, Spencer, their older brother Tom, and Reverend McCallie convened in the upstairs study of the father's home. They, along with sister Grace, who was absent, represented the five incorporators and directors of the school. Papers had already been filed chartering McCallie School as a for-profit corporation, a status that unfortunately would encumber the school's fund-raising efforts in the years ahead. Reverend McCallie was elected chairman of the corporation, Park secretary-treasurer, and Tom vice president.

At their meeting, the directors voted to create $50,000 in capital stock and sell it to Reverend McCallie in return for title to his home and 40-acre property, further proof of the father's wholehearted belief in his sons' endeavor. The Reverend kept $28,000 worth of the stock and divided the rest among the four: Park and Spencer receiving $10,000 in stock each; Tom and Grace receiving stock worth $1,000 each. Realizing the immediate need to build a dedicated school building to replace the house that had been converted to classrooms the first school year, the directors met a month later to borrow $12,000 from Reverend McCallie at six percent interest. A year later, he was issued $12,000 in preferred stock.

The first school year ended in June 1906 with a field day and oratorical contest instead of a traditional graduation. The commencement program in part recognized the work of Len White. Respected by students for both his scholarship and athleticism, White had successfully gained their acceptance of the McCallie Literary Society, which he established earlier in the year. He demonstrated that the art of debate and oration were masculine endeavors, as vigorous in their own way as sports. His society spawned a growing number of literary societies that came to involve every boy in school. Meeting once a week, they took turns debating, declaiming and "reading aloud in an interesting manner," activities designed to produce influential speakers.

The June exercise ended a banner first year, with seniors bound for Washington & Lee, Auburn, Cumberland University and the University of Virginia. The McCallie brothers were anticipating a busy summer constructing a school building and recruiting a second-year class. For Spencer, there was also love in the air. In August he married Alice Fletcher of Chattanooga. They would have five children, including a future headmaster of McCallie. But for now, the fledgling school was his baby, and it showed every sign of growth. The Chattanooga News, reporting on the school's first year, declared that "this child of education has walked away from some of its older competitors in its very infancy."

The brick School Building, constructed in 1906 to replace the frame house used for classes in 1905, appears at the far left of the page across McCallie Lake. Next to it is Founder's Home.

During the summer of 1906, Park McCallie was approached by Harlow Gates, a young man who lived in the East Lake community near school. Gates was attracted to McCallie by its Honor System and by the three-story, brick-and-concrete school building he saw rising on a terrace cut into the Ridge. He wanted to attend the school, but his family lacked the means.

"I had an idea," Gates recalled years later. "I told Doctor Park we couldn't afford tuition, but the school had windows to be washed, floors to be swept and oiled, and, in the winter, a furnace to be fired. I told him I could do all those things in lieu of tuition. 'Young man,' said Doctor Park, 'you have a job, and we have a scholar.'"

Though parents of the vast majority of boys attending McCallie paid full tuition, there were talented boys that the school assisted with aid in its earliest days and in the decades to follow. Russell Tate, who graduated in 1929 with the Grayson Medal as the most highly regarded boy in school, was an example. Tate's father died when Tate was entering the eighth grade at McCallie, leaving his stepmother unable to pay for private schooling.

"Doctor told me to see him," said Tate, "and see if we could make arrangements where I could continue at McCallie." They did, with Tate work-

ing off tuition by cleaning classrooms in the early morning, serving in the cafeteria at lunchtime, helping in the recorder's office and the carpentry staff after athletics, and working on the campus in summertime.

More than 90 students enrolled for McCallie's second year. They attended classes in the new $12,000 school building above Kyle Street. Boarders roomed in Founder's Home and the frame house that had been a makeshift school building the first year. Grace McCallie, meanwhile, was accepting 45 girls in the newly opened Girls' Preparatory School located in her home on Oak Street. The McCallie brothers had donated used desks to the school, as Grace and cofounders Eula Jarnagin and Tommie Duffy emulated what the McCallie brothers had accomplished a year before by establishing GPS in three-months time.

The first issue of the McCallie Pennant was published in late April 1907. It was established as a monthly magazine of student essays, poems, humor and news. The spring issue doubled as the year-end review and would soon

The 1907-08 Pennant staff was the second to produce the school publication. Conceived as a literary periodical, it soon became the McCallie annual. The staff announced the intention to create a student publication that would compare favorably with the best in the country.

evolve into the school annual. The inaugural issue reported on a fire that destroyed the frame dorm on the afternoon of April 10. No students were hurt, though Spencer twisted an ankle when knocked from the roof by a fire extinguisher's blast, and Park sustained a badly bruised nose when struck by an iron bed flung from a second-story window. The Pennant took a jocular view of the proceedings, poking fun at the bungling attempts by teachers and students to fight the fire, and declaring: "The dear old shack is no more!"

Tragic, though, was the death, also in April 1907, of Len White. The promising 21-year-old teacher died of peritonitis a month after organizing the McCallie School Dramatic Club. "Now that he is gone," a saddened Park McCallie wrote in a memorial to White in the Pennant, "and he no more instructs from the open book, we see that his life was an open book to us, and that we were learning from him by lessons far more powerful than the spoken word." The McCallie Literary Society was renamed Len White Literary Society in his honor.

Douglas Hall dormitory, at left, was built in 1907, with a third floor added in 1916. In 1919, North and South Halls were added to the School Building, which then became known as Middle Hall. Until 1919, the campus consisted of the two building above, Founder's Home and the small gym built in 1905.

With the loss of the frame building and a record enrollment of 110 students expected for the fall 1907 term, the headmasters needed dormitory space. That summer they borrowed $6,000 and added a $5,000 loan from an unnamed benefactor to construct brick, two-story Douglas Hall on Kyle Street. Named for the family of Reverend McCallie's wife, Ellen, it accommodated 35 boys and also served as the headmasters' office and Park's residence. His wife,

Hattie, planted a rose garden on the hillside outside the dorm where a strawberry patch also thrived. The three-story academic building sitting higher up the Ridge, Founder's Home just above it and the small gym near the lake would, along with Douglas Hall, comprise all the buildings of the McCallie School campus until 1919. That year the academic building would be enlarged by adding the North Hall and South Hall wings.

The teaching staff, on the other hand, was in flux. The school was attracting young college men getting their first taste of the classroom. For many of them, McCallie was a training ground for positions of leadership at other schools. George Briggs was an example. A graduate of Southwestern Presbyterian University, he arrived at McCallie in 1907 as a teacher and coach. He would remain six years before going to Darlington School in Rome, GA, then to Baylor, and finally to Battle Ground Academy in Franklin, TN, where he served 19 years as headmaster. As happened with new teachers at McCallie in its early days, Briggs, a Latin specialist, was asked to teach whatever class needed an instructor. "When my brother, in a pinch, asked him to teach an arithemetic class," recalled Park McCallie, "he (Briggs) cried, 'Professor, ...I can't add two and two and get four.'"

Latin and Greek instructor George Briggs also coached baseball and football at McCallie from 1907 to 1914, helping establish the school's winning athletic tradition. He later served as headmaster at Battle Ground Academy in Franklin TN.

In McCallie's first four years of existence, 125 boys had attended the school for a year or more and approximately 40 had entered college. With this base of support, McCallie in the fall of 1909 established an alumni association, which hosted its first annual banquet at the Hotel Patten. Some 50 graduates attended the event on the Monday evening after Christmas, and spirit in the room was high. That fall, George Briggs had coached the football team to a 4-1 record, defeating arch rivals Baylor 28-0 and City High 22-0. To the distress of alumni, Briggs was now considering leaving McCallie. With a flair for the dramatic, Spencer McCallie jumped up in the middle of dinner and read a pur-

POST CARD

THIS SPACE FOR WRITING MESSAGES

McCallie 5 Sewanee Mil. 2
McCallie 0 Butler(H'ntsv'le) 5
McCallie 22 Baker Himel 2
McCallie 28 Baylor 0
McCallie 22 Chatta. High 0

The school's 1909 football team compiled a 4-1 record including a shutout of arch-rival Baylor. A postcard celebrated the season. The team's success was toasted at the first McCallie Alumni Association meeting held at the downtown Hotel Patten in December 1909.

ported telegram from Briggs. "I am certain," it declared, "to be with McCallie for the years 1910 and 1911 with another winning team." The unverified news set off a round of cheers at the tables and choruses of college yells.

Briggs, in fact, did stay to coach the 1910 team, which lost only one game and closed the season with an 18-0 victory over Baylor. But he left in the spring of 1911, and that fall McCallie fielded an exceptionally undersized team that was held scoreless in losing all five games of the season. So outclassed was the team, said the Pennant, that even Baylor seemed to "feel no elation" in its first win ever over McCallie, a 32-0 drubbing.

By the more important measures of enrollment and college placement, McCallie was winning. The large campus, the lake, which had become an aquatic amusement park with towering slides, swings and a toboggan-like chute, and the school spirit were all driving boys to McCallie, and the caliber of its college preparation was demonstrated by the schools that welcomed graduates. Members of the Class of 1910 attended Cornell, Virginia, Washington and Lee, Yale and Georgia Tech.

McCallie opened a primary department for fifth and sixth graders in the fall of 1910 under the direction of faculty member Louis Lester. Upperclassmen nick-named the young students "Little Shavers."

The Southern Association of Colleges and Schools had accredited McCallie in 1909. In fall 1910, the school, which had already begun admitting seventh and eighth graders, established a primary department for fifth and sixth graders, known as "Little Shavers." The school began offering summer programs, and Spencer McCallie escorted a handful of seniors on summer jaunts to Europe, touring England, France, Belgium and Holland by auto in 1908 and attending the coronation of England's King George V in 1911.

The arrival of Alexander Guerry in the fall of 1910 further strengthened McCallie's faculty. The 19-year-old Guerry had been the youngest graduate of the University of the South, where his father was chaplain. Guerry was "a brilliant teacher," said Park McCallie, "well-beloved by boys and faculty." Like George Briggs, Guerry was asked by the headmasters to teach a subject unfamiliar to him, German, and was assured he needed to stay only a lesson ahead of the class to be successful. Guerry was dismayed to learn on the first day in the classroom that one of his students had lived eight years in Germany.

Guerry had the drive and ability to be a leader in education, and like other highly capable and ambitious men who followed him at McCallie, he determined there wasn't room at the Ridge school for him to rise to the top. Baylor, on the other hand, was fertile ground. The school, led by an aging principal, was attracting barely more than a third of McCallie's enrollment, which by 1913 had soared to 140. Given the challenge of reviving Baylor, Guerry left McCallie in 1913 to become Baylor's athletic director and to teach. He would oversee that school's resurgence after its move to a new campus on the Tennessee River in 1915.

S pencer and Park handed major responsibility to another teacher, Clarence Wilcox. A Davidson graduate, Wilcox joined McCallie's faculty in 1911, left in 1918 to serve in World War I, and returned to McCallie as associate headmaster from 1919 to 1921. He was the first of a line of men who would assist the headmasters in the school's daily management. Wilcox continued his career as president of Darlington School in Rome, GA and was elected president of the Mid-South Association of Private Schools. Ever a friend of McCallie, he wrote fund-raising appeals for the school while at Darlington and returned to the Chattanooga campus as featured speaker for a dormitory dedication.

Joy and sadness mingled in the lives of the McCallies. Anne, the daughter of Park and Hattie, and Spencer, Jr., the first son of Alice and Spencer, were born in 1909. But Park and Hattie McCallie's son, Park Jr., died of diphtheria in Douglas Hall in September 1911. Park McCallie held his six-year-old son in his arms as the youngster gasped for air, calling the death "the greatest tragedy of my life." Hattie, meanwhile, was pregnant with Robert, who was born one

In the school's early days, McCallie's baseball team played on Alumni Field, football games were played on Patten Field near McCallie Lake, and basketball was played in the tiny 60' x 30' gym dubbed the "Dog House."

month later. The shock of delivering one child so soon after losing another took a temporary toll on her physical and emotional health. The following spring, on April 30, 1912, the patriarch of the McCallie family, Reverend Thomas H. McCallie, died in Founder's Home at age 74. He and his wife, Ellen, had celebrated their 50th anniversary three months before, and the entire family had gathered on campus to mark the occasion.

In 1913 and 1914, Park McCallie took a sabbatical from his duties as co-headmaster to tour Japan, China, Korea and other countries as stewardship secretary for the Foreign Mission Board of the Southern Presbyterian Church. His party, including his 73-year-old mother, Ellen, was detained for a time in Russia, which they entered in August 1914 as war in Europe was declared. But the tour ended safely, America avoided involvement for three more years, and, as Park rejoined Spencer, the school continued to grow. A third floor was added to Douglas Hall in 1916 and Alumni Field was dedicated the same year — its squared-off fifth-mile cinder track, tennis courts and outdoor gym built at a cost of $10,000.

By the spring of 1917, however, the United States had been drawn into the conflict that broadened into the First World War. A small force of 128,000 soldiers comprised the country's standing army at the time. As draftees were quickly trained and shipped overseas, feelings ran high that schools like McCallie needed to offer rudimentary military training, principally close-order drill, as an act of preparedness for the duration of the war.

Though Park McCallie originally planned for a day school, boarders were part of the student mix from the first enrolled class. Here, students study in a room at the turreted end of Founder's Home. Douglas Hall and South Hall, which was built in 1919, comprised the rest of McCallie's early residential community.

Chattanoogans celebrated the armistice of World War One in November 1918 by dancing in the streets. Along with other schools in the nation, McCallie adopted a military program that same year after the shortage of trained soldiers for the war effort revealed America's lack of military preparedness. Military training, however, was never a core element of the school's mission.

By 1918, McCallie had organized a battalion of two companies, with cadets dressed in olive uniforms and carrying rifles. Instead of retiring military training after the war ended in November 1918, the headmasters continued it as conducive to pride, patriotism and leadership development. They distinguished, however, between McCallie's confinement of military to wearing a uniform and setting aside a daily drill period and schools that were full-blown military academies, where students roomed in barracks and lived the regimented life of cadets around the clock. At McCallie, military was an adornment to education; academics came first.

J oyous Chattanoogans filled the downtown streets in the early morning hours after word reached America from Europe that on November 11, 1918, Germany had signed an armistice ending World War I. Spencer McCallie woke his daughter, Mary, and sons, Spencer Jr. and Thomas Hooke II, at 3 a.m. and piled them in his Model T to witness the event. "They (residents) were running up and down the street," recalls T. Hooke McCallie of "the ruckus that was going on," firing pistols and shotguns in the air, "going wild over the end of the war."

The McCallie Battalion stands at present arms in front of the school building as it appeared after construction of North and South Halls in 1919. During a short visit to the city in 1920, the commander of allied forces during World War I, General John "Black Jack" Pershing, inspected the battalion — a point of pride for the school.

The celebration was tempered by the loss of six McCallie alumni who died in the fighting. Among them was school standout Clifford Barker Grayson. Elected president of the McCallie YMCA and twice elected president of the Student Senate, he subsequently graduated from Cornell and Harvard Law School. He died in a French hospital on July 19, 1918 after being shot by a German machine gunner in the Second Battle of the Marne. His father, Judge D.L. Grayson of Chattanooga, established the Clifford Barker Grayson Memorial Medal in 1919 to honor the senior each year who would be most missed by the school. Judge Grayson personally presented the award through 1944.

Two weeks after the tumultuous celebration, grief struck Spencer McCallie's family as his wife, Alice, suddenly succumbed to double pneumonia from the deadly influenza epidemic sweeping the world. It would eventually claim more lives than the bloody war just ended. The couple had been married 12 years and had five children, Alice and Ellen being the youngest. In May 1920, the 44-year-old widowed headmaster married 26-year-old Katharine Pierce, a Pennsylvania native who was working at First Presbyterian Church. McCallie students avidly followed the courtship, and each donated a penny to buy the marriage license. David McCallie, who would become school physician and board chairman, was the child of their marriage.

As the school entered the 1920s, enrollment eclipsed 300 for the first time. To accommodate the surge in attendance, the McCallies added North and South wings to the academic building in the fall of 1919. The South Wing, as well as rooms created from the attic of Founder's Home, helped accommodate boarders attending from a dozen states. The third floor of North Hall would serve as a combination chapel, assembly room, study hall and drama stage until the school chapel was built in 1955. Hung above the stage at the front of the room on a varnished mahogany plaque inscribed in old English lettering was the 400-year-old answer to the first question of the Presbyterian Westminster Shorter Catechism: "Man's Chief End Is To Glorify God And To Enjoy Him Forever."

McCallie seemed uniquely able to combine bedrock belief with the educational preparation the modern world demanded of a young man. The school, in fact, performed an unusual series of balancing acts. It offered Christian training, yet was non-sectarian in policy, enrolling Jewish and Catholic as well as Protestant students. It provided military instruction but made clear it was not a military school. And privately, it was a for-profit corporation that never issued a dividend to its shareholders, as money earned was plowed back into the school and more was borrowed to keep it afloat.

Creating the glue that held the school together was the selfless commitment of the two founders and of the faculty and staff who took up their cause. Their dedication would lead McCallie through one of its most difficult periods that lay a decade ahead.

As the 1920s dawned, Park and Spencer McCallie's dream of a Southern school that would prepare boys well for higher education had fully materialized. Alumni were enrolled in some of the best universities in the Ivy League and the South, and the school's reputation was widely recognized in educational circles.

Chapter Three

Feast and Famine

1921-1940

T HE SECOND-FLOOR NORTH HALL class resembled a Norman Rockwell tableau: twelve-year-old boys hunched forward at their desks, eyes and mouths wide open. They had reason for gawking. Their bald, 46-year-old teacher had just opened the morning period with a flat-footed leap from the floor to the top of his sturdy, oak desk. Now with the eyes of students riveted on him, he stood on the floor before them, his own eyes wide, brandishing an eraser and flailing it in the air. Everywhere he turned were Philistines, and he was meting out punishment worthy of the Bible's most powerful warrior. With grunts and moans to the back row he fought. Soon, the battlefield before him was littered with the slain, and Spencer McCallie, flashing a triumphant smile, put down what passed for the jawbone of an ass. Cheers erupted, and the laughter and applause of boys spilled from the windows of the rambling brick school building on the Ridge.

In the autumn of 1921, McCallie School reverberated with the vitality of "Fessor" McCallie and the optimism of the nation. The war to end all wars had been fought and won, and a golden age of American prosperity was underway. The school mirrored the ebullient times. Enrollment had climbed to 300, and the campus hummed with energy. It was felt in the between-class commotion of the student body and in the teaching of a maturing faculty; in orders barked by upperclassmen on the drill field and in the roar from the stands as the school's football juggernaut rolled to an undefeated season.

By the school's sixteenth year, Spencer and his brother, Park, had been successful in achieving their goals of offering boys college preparation, physical development and Christian training. The importance of the latter was under-  scored by the fact that Bible instruction was reserved for the two headmasters and the school's new asso- ciate headmaster, Thomas Edward Peck Woods. Initially offered as an all-but-mandatory elective, Bible had become, by 1919, a diploma require- ment. T.E.P. Woods taught Old Testament in the intermediate grades and chaired the department,

The student body surrounds McCallie Lake in 1926. In the background at right is the concrete gymnasium, built in 1924, and the small wooden gym built by the founders in 1905. A portion of the campus of McCallie's public school neighbor, Central High, is on the left. The concrete diving platform still stands, making it the oldest structure on campus.

An aerial view of the campus in the early 1930's shows the academic building, Douglas Hall, Founder's Home and the two gyms. At lower center is Alumni Field, encircled by a fifth-mile track. The field would be moved northward in 1934 to accommodate a quarter-mile cinder track. At the picture's bottom-right edge is Patten Field, where the city's first night football game was played in 1930.

and Park taught New Testament to seniors.

Spencer McCallie's Old Testament class was one of the school's most memorable courses. It mattered not if the subject was Samson and his exploits, or Jacob wrestling the angel until dawn, or God turning Lot's disobedient wife to a pillar of salt, Spencer knew how to rivet the attention of seventh- and eighth-grade students. Acting out tales with bravura, he turned the ten plagues into a cliff-hanging serial and invented humorous contemporary dialogue for 3,000-year-old stories. The effect was to sear Biblical images into the minds of hundreds of McCallie boys for a lifetime.

In other ways, too, Christian influence was woven through McCallie life. The Pocket Testament League, a campus organization, presented students who joined with small editions of the New Testament they pledged to carry and read from daily. Evangelists, including the renowned Billy Sunday, spoke at student devotionals, and weeklong revivals were held each fall and spring. Boarders attended church on Sunday mornings and participated in religious-oriented YMCA programs in Douglas Hall on Sunday nights. Through the YMCA, they collected money to help Christian schools in China and Japan, anticipating the efforts of the Missionary Committee, which would be formed in 1939. Park McCallie packaged his daily announcements in the form of informational prayers and presided over the saying of grace at evening meals.

The recruitment of T.E.P. Woods reflected the school's practice of selecting faculty for "Christian character and influence as well as for their ability as teachers." The veteran churchman and schoolman filled a critical vacuum created by the departure of Associate Headmaster Clarence Wilcox for Darlington in 1921. "The McCallie School has grown so rapidly in the last three years," wrote a beleaguered Spencer to Woods that year, "that there is a great need for more strong and experienced men in the Faculty, as the burdens are becoming too heavy for J.P. and me."

Woods brought to McCallie the credentials of an ordained minister, a Latin, Greek and Bible scholar, an author of religious books, a poet and a school principal. He had attended Southwestern Presbyterian University in Clarksville, TN as a classmate of Spencer, then earned a doctor of divinity degree

--- ◆◆◆ ---

The school's greatest natural asset was McCallie Lake, which provided recreation for students and needed income for the school from bathers who paid to swim and use the bathhouse in the summer months. For a time, the lake offered a Coney Island-array of towers, swings and slides and, at the right, a 30-foot-high, 100-foot-long toboggan run, as viewed from the top of it.

--- ◆◆◆ ---

from Union Theological Seminary and Presbyterian School of Christian Education in Richmond, VA. He had pastored three churches and served as head of four schools including, most recently, a North Carolina academy that had been destroyed by fire.

A small, spindly man with a slew-footed gait, he cast a large shadow across McCallie's campus. A strict disciplinarian as well as versatile teacher, he would become the headmasters' ramrod in regulating student behavior through the complex Privilege Rating System he devised. His daughter, Zella, would be his helpmate in the endeavor as the school's meticulous and reclusive recorder of grades and demerits. While a quick temper and a stern, pursed-lip demeanor made T.E.P. Woods an intimidating figure, his devotion to the

The school's drum-and-bugle corps stands at the main entrance on McCallie Avenue in 1928. For decades, motorists entering McCallie had to turn off of the busy thoroughfare, and the school had to live with city-owned Kyle Street traversing the campus. Not until 1994, after the school purchased neighboring property that expanded the campus and secured its borders, was the main entrance moved to Dodds Avenue and Kyle became a school-owned street.

school, his penchant for befriending boys in special need of help, and the gradual softening of his personality to reveal "a subtle humor," as the Pennant described it, endeared him to many during his 27 years at McCallie.

Frances Thornton Strang brought a different dimension to the faculty. A graduate of Columbia University in New York City, she was an unexpected gift of the First World War, when male teachers were in such short supply that McCallie was agreeable to hiring a highly qualified female instructor. She joined the faculty in 1918 and immediately elevated the standards of the English department as chairman. She introduced the use of biographical research in understanding a writer's work, campaigned for an adequate library and brought literature to life in the classroom. In the process, she earned the respect and affection of students, who dedicated the 1920 Pennant in her honor. At her death in February 1922, she bequeathed the school her own book collection and a sum of money for the development of the library department.

By the early 1920s, McCallie had eight literary societies that met for a 45-minute period on Fridays and involved every student in debates and other forms of public speaking that polished communications skills. The remainder of the week, the period was assigned to military drill and calisthenics on Alumni Field. Dressed in brown serge uniforms and leather puttees, cadets were divided into three companies: "A", which represented McCallie in the

Doctor Park McCallie, in straw hat, often led students on a popular outing to Umbrella Rock on Lookout Mountain. **Park and Spencer McCallie** promoted Chattanooga's rugged and scenic beauty to attract boarding students from across the South.

annual drill competition with Baylor, City High and Central High at Warner Park; "B" comprised of students less experienced in the manual of arms; and "C" for grammar-school-age "Little Shavers," who carried light, wooden rifles. Over time, more companies would be added, and the battalion would become a regiment.

Whether in oratorical contests, drill tournaments or athletics, McCallie thrived on competition and missed few opportunities to proclaim its achievements. For example, McCallie boasted of being the only school in Chattanooga inspected by General John "Black Jack" Pershing, commander of American forces in World War I, during his brief visit to the city in 1920. In truth, the general's impromptu inspection of the McCallie battalion was the result of the school's location along his motorcade route and an opportunistic corps of cadets that stood at attention and saluted as the general approached, encouraging the war hero to add the school to his itinerary.

Spirit on the football field ran particularly high. For the first 15 years, McCallie's athletic teams were known by the school colors: "The Blue and White." Coach Hal Blair's dominating 1921 football squad was the first to be called "Blue Tornado," aptly describing a team that compiled a 7-0 record in a series of blowouts, outscoring opponents 271-6. The team, whose heaviest player weighed 170 pounds, was led by Andrew "Scrappy" Moore, a 138-pound junior and All-City end. If not size, then age and experience were factors in McCallie's success. Fielding postgraduates, the team included two 20-year-olds and four 19-year-olds. More than a dozen players had earned varsity letters at other schools before transferring to McCallie.

After holding the first six teams on the schedule scoreless, McCallie faced an equally talented and experienced Baylor team in the traditional season finale for the two private schools. McCallie prevailed 12-6, breaking a three-year string of losses to Baylor in a ballyhooed annual rivalry that engaged the entire city. Game week was marked by daily sports-page articles as well as motorcades, bonfires, public graffiti and campus raids. The game was held on the Saturday afternoon before Thanksgiving and played at the University of Chattanooga's Chamberlain Field since neither school's stadium could accommodate the more than 5,000 spectators who regularly attended. Odds were set downtown, and wagers were made. Afterward, fans of the winning team would stage exuberant snake dances through department stores and streets. "There was a lot of intense feeling in those days," said Frank Thompson, a day student who played as a 136-pound end some years later in 1933. "The Baylor game was an all-out, bust-a-gut deal."

McCallie's larger reputation was in academics, and the school's prestige received a boost when Spencer was elected president of the Southern Association of Colleges and Secondary Schools for the 1922-23 year. His leadership in educational and civic circles, including speeches to Kiwanis Clubs across the South, helped attract day and boarding students. So did Park's involvement with religious organizations and causes, from the Chattanooga Plan of Bible Study in the Public Schools, which he spearheaded, to foreign mission board work for the Southern Presbyterian Church, which he had

⊷ ⬩ ⊶

chaired. Park's strong church ties in North Carolina drew students from the Tarheel State, and his teaching stint at Culver enabled McCallie to become a charter member of the Independent Schools of the Central States. Both men gave the school visibility among parents seeking both strong college preparation and Christian education for their sons. The result was a continued growth in enrollment that by 1925 had reached 320.

McCallie's good name made it possible for the headmasters to recruit talented instructors, many of whom would launch distinguished careers at McCallie. English Department Director Henry Lilly would become a highly respected Davidson College professor of English, and Lee Sager, who headed McCallie's mathematics department for 20 years, would become headmaster of Montgomery Bell Academy in Nashville. George Griffin, athletics director and varsity football and track coach, would become dean of students at Georgia Tech; Latin teacher R.F. "Tommy" Thomason would become registrar for the University of Tennessee; and English department head William Tate, who joked that his grandfather was the only private in the Confederate Army, would become the longtime dean of men at the University of Georgia.

But 1925 saw a reversal of the trend of making McCallie a way-stop for talented educators. That fall, four young men joined the faculty who would dedicate their lives to the school, providing continuity and stability during uncertain times, such as the one fast approaching, and shaping the McCallie experience for decades of students.

⸺⸺ ⊷ ⬩ ⊶ ⸺⸺

Chalmers McIlwaine was the skinny, 10-year-old son of Presbyterian missionaries living in the Japanese coastal town of Kochi on the island of Shikoku when Park McCallie visited the family in 1914 during a worldwide tour with his mother on behalf of the Southern Presbyterian Church. Before Park left the McIlwaines, he conveyed the hope that Chalmers and his older brother would attend McCallie School one day. The low-key recruitment effort yielded the first of two dozen sons of missionaries who would come to McCallie over the next twenty years from half a world away.

By 1919, Chalmers McIlwaine was enrolled as a sophomore at McCallie. Arriving in Chattanooga the summer before his first semester, the energetic McIlwaine earned spending money by carrying water to construction workers building North and South Halls and spent his free time watching the Lookouts

minor league baseball team from the wooden stands at Andrews Field, later renamed Engel Stadium.

One year ahead of McIlwaine at McCallie School was Arthur Lee Burns. Where McIlwaine was eagerly involved in activities as a winning debater, a literary society officer and an elected dormitory monitor called a Prefect, Burns maintained a lower profile during four years at McCallie. "He is quiet and manly in bearing and commands the respect of all who know him," said the Pennant in its senior-year summary of Burns. The cultured Burns, who loved classical music and opera with the passion McIlwaine reserved for sports, enrolled at Emory University where he earned bachelor's and master's degrees in French. McIlwaine went to Davidson College, where he edited the student newspaper and briefly considered a career in journalism.

The two were reunited in 1925 after accepting offers from Spencer McCallie to return to their growing alma mater to teach. They were joined by Herbert Dunlap, a rural South Carolinian with a pronounced drawl and courtly Southern manners, who had just graduated with top-cadet honors from the Citadel in Charleston. He applied to McCallie after hearing a chapel announcement that the Chattanooga school needed an English and American history teacher and assistant comman-dant. The fourth pillar of the faculty to arrive that fall was Wallace Purdy, a classmate of McIlwaine at

At top: Wallace Purdy, conducting an experiment in chemistry class, led the school's science department for three decades. At center, boarders in the late 1920's took a meal at the dining room located in South Hall. The study hall, located on the third floor of North Hall, is pictured around 1930.

Davidson. Purdy's dubious claim to fame to that point was his forcing the quarantining of the Davidson campus after contracting smallpox. The four were hired at $140 a month plus room, board and laundry, and there was nothing at the time to signal the school had scored a recruitment bonanza. But long before they contributed a collective 174 years of teaching and administrative talent to McCallie, they would be regarded as legends.

⋯⋯ ✦✦✦ ⋯⋯

During the flush years of the 1920s, the McCallie brothers continued to plow money from tuition into the school's physical plant, with athletic facilities receiving special attention. A major addition to the campus was a large, cement-block gymnasium built near the lake in 1924 to replace the school's cramped gym, known as the "doghouse," that had been in use since 1905. The new, barn-like structure with a maple-wood court enabled Park to boast of the school having "the best gymnasium in the city."

Patten Field, offering bleachers for football games, was developed west of the gym in 1928. The result of the generosity of the Patten brothers, Zeboim and George, the funding of the field was an exception to the school's general inability to attract private gifts for capital projects. A 1925 Alumni Association campaign to raise $100,000 for McCallie, including $60,000 for a chapel that was of heartfelt importance to Park, yielded only $18,000. As the school was learning repeatedly, alumni were reluctant to make non-tax-deductible contributions to a privately-owned, for-profit organization, even one they revered.

School spirit, though, was strong as McCallie entered its 25th year in the fall of 1929. T.E.P. Woods was implementing the complex rating system he designed to govern student life. It weighed grades, general deportment, attendance, athletic participation, military behavior and school activities to determine each student's two-week class rating, A through E, and the privileges or penalties that accrued. The system, said the school, encouraged boys not to measure themselves against others but to "do their best."

That same year, Arthur Burns was developing a more lighthearted tradition by penning the words to the Alma Mater that first appeared in print in the 1930 Pennant. He would personally teach the challenging tune each year during a student assembly, admonishing boys not to scream the final refrain's "Hail, all hail," which they took delight in doing. Of the "melodic contraption" that was the Alma Mater, McCallie historian George Hazard wrote: "No one liked it, no one would junk it."

Another established tradition was that of family legacies. Harry Durand, Jr. '28 had become the first second-generation McCallie graduate. His father had attended the school from 1906 to 1909. The headmasters' own sons were also recent graduates: Spencer Jr. in 1928 and Robert in 1929. They had been reared on a campus that to a youngster was as much a farm as an academy. Horses pulled a surrey, and two mules were hitched to mowers to keep the campus trimmed. Vegetables raised in the garden were served in the dining room, milk from the cows was put on the table, and an orchard on the hill above the school building provided fruit for canning, though students filched ripe apples, pears and peaches from the trees and threw rotten ones at one another.

The roaring '20s came to a shocking halt in October 1929 with the crash of the New York Stock Exchange. Panicked stockholders sold a record 16.4 million shares in one day, ushering in the Great Depression. Stock values continued to sink for the next three years as the national economy floundered. By 1933, almost 9,000 banks had closed, prices of industrial stocks had fallen 80 percent, and one-quarter of the labor force, 13 million people, were without a job. Many were dispossessed of their homes, and soup lines and hobo jungles sprang up as part of the American landscape.

The effect on McCallie was a precipitous decline in enrollment. It plummeted from 316 students in grades seven through twelve in fall 1929 (5th and

---

Activities abounded at McCallie, from literary societies to a hunting club. Members of the travel club are shown in the mid-1920's.

For years, Professor Spencer McCallie was faculty advisor to the Student Senate, which investigated Honor Code violations. During the Senate's 1929 term, he is flanked on his right by his nephew, Robert McCallie, the school's future co-headmaster, and on his left by Russell Tate, who would become the school's junior school principal and athletic director.

6th grades had been eliminated in the middle of the decade) to a low of 190 students (97 day and 93 boarding) in fall 1932. The school hadn't admitted that few boarders since 1918, and it would be 1938 before the school's total enrollment reached the high-water mark of the 1920's.

To survive the period, McCallie put key personnel on the road throughout the summer months, scouring Tennessee and surrounding states for a shrinking pool of families with the means to send their sons to a private boarding school. McIlwaine and Dunlap joined the headmasters in making the trips. "When we went out recruiting," said McIlwaine, "we were looking for boys with athletic ability as well as academic ability. To tell the truth," he added, of the difficult times, "we were looking for boys."

False leads, poor directions and uncertain lodgings, particularly when venturing into small towns, were hazards of the exhausting assignment. In the drilling heat of summer, Dunlap traveled Alabama and Mississippi in his Model-T Ford. The South's gravel backroads presented him a particular challenge. "Those big rocks would fly up and knock your windshield out," he recalled years later. Reluctant to ask the cash-strapped school for reimbursement, he bore the cost of repairs from his $4 daily allowance. To further pare travel expenses, he stayed, when invited, in the homes of alumni or of the prospects themselves.

The grip of the Depression was unrelenting, and Park McCallie, who acted as treasurer, used various means to keep the school afloat. He and Spencer borrowed against personal life insurance policies. The school earned money from summer concessions at McCallie Lake, where residents took the Number Four trolley and paid 35 cents for a locker and wire basket to swim at the popular recreational spot.

Park found a bargain for redeveloping Alumni Field. The work of leveling a ten-foot rise in order to move the playing field northward, of erecting stone

By the 1930's, military was rooted in McCallie life, even though the school was never a full-fledged military academy. At top, sponsors for the regimental officers prepare to review the cadets. Alumni Field, at center and bottom, was the location for daily drill and full-dress parades. Herbert Dunlap, the school commandant, started the annual Mother's Day parade in 1933.

bleachers on the east side and of constructing a quarter-mile cinder track was performed for a modest $5,000 by the federal WPA in 1934 with the stipulation that McCallie make the field available to the public for softball games in the summer. "The school would have been lost during the Depression," declared Bill Pressly, a future headmaster at McCallie, "if not for Doctor's ability to make a dollar go a long way."

In 1932, with McCallie's enrollment at low ebb and the school struggling to meet expenses, Spencer and Park turned to the staff for help. Dunlap recalled Park's address to the faculty. "'We've just got to tighten our belts,' Doctor told us," said Dunlap. 'Professor and I are both taking 20 percent cuts in our salaries. We

appreciate our faculty and want all of you to stay with us, but we're going to ask you to take a 20 percent cut as we've done.'" There was silence in the room. "Not any member of the staff left," said Dunlap. "We all stayed."

Their sacrifice was considerable. Cuts would exceed 20 percent before the school regained its financial footing, and it would be decades before the salaries that teachers lost during that era began to be made up. In the view of T. Hooke McCallie, the school "was close to being a non-entity. The faculty's stand," he said, "has always been an emotional thing to me." The willingness of the faculty to work for meager pay and the headmasters to "live close to poverty," as Spencer, Jr. described it, enabled the school to survive. Dunlap, though, saw a silver lining in the difficult years. "The fact we went through the Depression together," he said, "brought us closer together."

Except for a shrunken enrollment and virtual absence of cars on campus, student life continued much as before. "We didn't feel the Depression at all," claimed Dr. Charles Sienknecht, who graduated in 1933 as a boarding student who hailed from a coal mining camp managed by his parents near Oak Ridge, TN. "Since we were all in uniform, any difference in family means didn't show." Professor would sometimes mention the Depression in assemblies, said Sienknecht, but days were filled with the customary classes, drill period, literary society debates and afternoon athletics.

On Saturday mornings, backwork drew boys struggling with classes and detention hauled in rule violators. A "mark" represented a set amount of time a student had to perform a task as punishment for an offense. To "work off" marks, older boys washed windows and cleaned blackboards, which they could reach, and smaller boys, armed with aluminum-handled GI knives, got on their knees to pry chewing gum from the pinewood floors. Harry Weill '32, a day student, was so accustomed to spending Saturday mornings at McCallie for marks received the previous week that he showed up once when he had not been called back. "Out of force of habit," he says in amusement at himself, "I took a knife and went to work on the floor anyway."

To balance the rigors of school life and respond to changing mores, the school's social life was broadened. Since its construction in 1924, the new gymnasium had been the site for coed gatherings, from Halloween socials, where Spencer read ghost stories, to roller skating parties. But not until 1933 were campus dances sanctioned, and then under strict supervision. They were heavily chaperoned by faculty, and a student was required to fill out a dance card so his date would meet other couples and not spend the evening in the arms of one boy.

By fall 1935, both Bob and Spencer, Jr., the sons of the headmasters and future co-headmasters themselves, were teaching at the school. After graduating from McCallie, both had enrolled at Davidson, where they roomed together. Bob graduated Phi Beta Kappa and as a Rhodes Scholarship candidate. Spencer Jr., known as Spence, transferred from

Early standouts of the faculty occupy the front row in this 1933 photograph. From left are: Capt. (later Col.) H.P. Dunlap, Spencer McCallie, Jr., Bill Tate, Arthur Lee Burns, T.E.P. Woods, Professor Spencer McCallie, Doctor Park McCallie, C.M.S. McIlwaine, Raulin Chambliss, Wallace Purdy, W.A. Venable and Eugene Hill. Bill Tate later served as a renowned dean at the University of Georgia.

Davidson to the University of Virginia, where he received his bachelor's degree. The cousins returned to McCallie for one-year teaching stints before earning master's degrees at Duke University. On their permanent return to the faculty, they joined Burns, Dunlap, McIlwaine and Purdy, all beginning their tenth year, and T.E.P. Woods, in his fourteenth. Bill Pressly, who would guide the school's English department, share headmaster duties with the two cousins for a short time, and marry into their family, arrived a year later.

Though the brute suffering of the Depression was easing and student enrollment at McCallie was slowly climbing, the school faced intractable financial problems from its for-profit status. It meant McCallie was doubly cursed: required to pay property and income taxes, yet unable to grant tax deductions that encouraged private gifts. Several times since 1922, Park had asked that

McCallie consider converting to a non-profit organization, as Baylor had done in 1914. But school attorneys consistently opposed the idea, advising, as attorney William Frierson did, that the McCallie family maintain complete control and ownership "until such time as later on our alumni become older and better able to take hold."

By 1937, that time had arrived. The school was saddled with debt that included money borrowed to expand Founder's Home to accommodate 22 additional students. Even with trimmed salaries, the school's dependence on tuition and fees alone to cover annual expenses left the brothers unable to plan for campus expansion and adequately service the debt. Baylor, meanwhile, had built a $40,000 chapel from alumni gifts, enlarged its library and gym, refur-

bished its dormitories, completed its quadrangle and established an endowment.

In January 1937, Park and Spencer received a $50,000 low-interest loan from Provident Life & Accident Insurance Company, whose president, Robert Maclellan, and his son, Bob '24, vice president, were strong supporters of the school. The consolidation loan, however, provided only temporary relief, and by the summer the school was having difficulty meeting payments.

In hopes of permanently remedying the school's precarious financial position, the McCallies took the long-discussed step of converting to non-profit status. A meeting of the school's board was convened on August 10, 1937 on the mezzanine floor of the Hotel Patten to consider the matter. In attendance were school attorney John Fletcher and board members Spencer; Park; Spencer, Jr.; Margaret McCallie, the headmasters' younger sister; Dr. J.L. Bibb, Park's brother-in-law and the school's longtime physician; and alumni representative Edward Brown '07. Robert McCallie was out of town.

The board immediately voted to seek a new charter as a non-profit educational corporation called The McCallie School and to transfer all school assets to a newly created board of trustees. This action, explained the board in its minutes, would enable the new corporation to "solicit the support of the public."

Jake Fine tackles Baylor's Henry Jumonville in McCallie's 21-7 victory in 1935. The postcard of school groundskeeper Laurence Potts with a mule painted by students was meant to inspire the team for the next year's campaign. Bill Spears '24, at left, was a small but nimble McCallie quarterback who became an All American at Vanderbilt University.

Three weeks later in a follow-up meeting in the office of Robert Maclellan at the Provident Building, the incorporators accepted the new charter, which had just been registered; adopted by-laws; elected Spencer and Park as headmasters and voted to pay them $25,000 in cash and an additional $100,000, divided evenly in 10-year and 20-year notes, for their ownership of the school's assets.

The conversion to non-profit status, formally approved a year later by the Internal Revenue Service, not only placed McCallie in a much better position to seek contributions from its 3,000 alumni but brought to the board men with the influence, knowledge and resources to guide the school's growth. Joining the members of the previous family board, who carried over their trustee membership, were Robert Maclellan, who was named vice president (Spencer and Park kept their titles as president and secretary-treasurer respectively), R.F. Thomason, John Hutcheson, Jr., Llewellyn Chapman, J.E. Millis, the Rev. G. Allen Fleece and Morgan Bright. Ed Chapin joined the board the following year.

Any fear that a private, non-profit board would usurp Spencer's or Park's authority to direct the school, as they had done successfully for 32 years, proved unfounded. "The board's focus was on achieving a tenable financial situation," explained McIlwaine. "They never tried to manage the operations of the school; they let the heads run it exactly as they had before." For 61-year-old Spencer, the private board also offered assurance to him and Park, 57, of the school having "a continuity of purpose and of life that it could not have under individual ownership."

To the 315 students enrolled in 1937 from 15 states and four foreign countries and the 25 members of the faculty and staff, little had changed at McCallie. Spencer was still displaying his physical vigor by jumping flat-footed to the top of his classroom desk, doing back somersaults from a giant swing into the lake and leading boys on hunting trips to South Georgia on Christmas break. Park was still scrutinizing invoices, teaching algebra and New Testament Bible and keeping a running tally of the Bible's translation into a growing number of the world's languages and dialects. Cadets, who now dressed in blue uniforms with white pants, were drawing up in ranks for the annual Mother's Day Parade, a tradition begun by Dunlap in 1933.

Remarkably, given the difficult times, McCallie not only sustained but built on its record of academic achievement. Selected as one of 200 schools to participate in a national analysis of secondary educational standards in 1938, McCallie received the study's "superior" rating. Two years later the school rated highest of any public or private Tennessee high school on the University of Tennessee's entrance examination. That same year, when more than 800 high school seniors in the South took the Emory University entrance exam, three of the top five test scores belonged to McCallie students.

The school maintained its prowess on the athletic field. In the 1920s, McCallie, blessed with foreign students who knew the game of soccer, introduced the sport to the area. During that decade, the school established wrestling and boxing teams, recorded a three-year streak of state track championships, and placed lights on Patten Field, which in October 1930 became the first in the area to host a night football game.

The Mid-South Association of Private Schools had been formed in 1932 to promote academics and athletics among member schools, and Spencer served as its first president. McCallie won the Mid-South football championship in 1933 with a 9-0-1 record that included a 13-0 defeat of Baylor. Knoxville native "Breezin" Bob Andridge, a powerful running back with sprinter speed, led McCallie to a 9-0 football season in 1936. The team outscored opponents 210-25 and beat previously undefeated Baylor 19-7, marking the first time since 1910 that McCallie had defeated Baylor two years in a row. The 1938 football team posted an 8-0-1 record, including a scoreless tie with Baylor.

The series with Baylor would be halted by McCallie in 1940 for 31 years,

however. Regardless of who won the annual game (and Baylor held the series advantage), McCallie officials felt that emotions surrounding it had reached an unhealthy pitch for high school athletics and diverted attention from academics and other aspects of school life. Passions were less volatile in other Mid-South Association sports, where the two schools continued to compete.

As 1940 arrived, the headmasters had both passed their 60th birthdays, having devoted the majority of those years to nurturing the institution that bore their name. With their guidance, the school had weathered the Depression, which had inadvertently strengthened it by forcing a change in its

- - ◆ - -

As the school's fourth decade approached, the McCallie brothers maintained their vigorous leadership. Professor McCallie is flanked by wife, Katharine, who was school librarian, and their son, David, who later served as school physician, trustee and chairman of the Board. Hattie McCallie, wife of Doctor Park McCallie, is honored at a school parade. At the right of the picture are Col. H.P. Dunlap and Doctor Park.

corporate structure. The joblessness that plagued the nation through the 1930's suddenly disappeared under the full employment needed to build and sustain America's fighting forces in World War II. Finding students was no longer a difficult summertime search; they were finding McCallie.

The lean years had tested the commitment and determination of the headmasters. Their father anticipated this trial when he told his sons in 1905 that running their own school "would develop both of you, especially if you had to struggle for awhile to get and keep the school on its feet." As a new decade opened, the school was more than still standing; it was racing to accommodate a surging enrollment. The 1940 student body of 348 students from 19 states and three foreign countries was the largest in school history, and it presaged a dramatic growth that would require an unprecedented response from the school's alumni and other benefactors to transform the small campus. It was a challenge that required a leap of faith that McCallie, by spiritual temperament and non-profit status, was now prepared to make.

The McCallie Board of Trustees provided the direction that enabled the school to thrive after it became a private, non-profit educational organization in 1937. The Board wisely left the school's management in the hands of the headmasters, a collaborative arrangement that brought the school steady success. Many stalwarts of the Board appear in this 1960's photograph.

Chapter Four

Growing Ambitions

1941-1960

I**N JUNE** 1941, at a meeting of the McCallie Board of Trustees in the downtown Provident Building office of Robert Maclellan '27, Spencer and Park McCallie read a polite but pointed letter. "Now that we are no longer owners of McCallie," the co-headmasters stated, "we are released from our former embarrassment in presenting McCallie's needs to its friends." They described the necessity to expand a campus straining to accommodate an enrollment that had grown by 80 percent since the bottom of the Depression in 1932. Immediately needed was a freestanding dining hall and cafeteria that would release space on the ground floor of South Hall for more classrooms. They noted that the Board had already authorized what it called the Greater McCallie Building Campaign to raise $100,000 for a dining hall as well as chapel, infirmary and addition to the concrete-block gym beside the lake but that little had been received beyond a modest but encouraging gift of a dollar each from the 100 seniors who graduated in May.

The brothers knew the school's lackluster record for attracting donations. In 1927, for example, a $100,000 drive to develop Alumni Field and make other campus improvements raised but $18,000. The picture had changed little since the school's adoption of non-profit status in 1937. In 1938, alumni provided a small structure to house a telescope that had been donated to the school, and the Lockett family of Knoxville presented the school a $6,000 check for a senior lounge, Lockett Lodge, that was built and dedicated in 1940. Otherwise, McCallie had always borrowed to build. "During all these years," stated Spencer and Park by comparison, "many other schools around McCallie have received gifts of new buildings and endowments amounting to hundreds

McCallie entered the 1940's with ambitious growth in mind. The 1941 master campus plan envisioned a chapel at the corner of Kyle Street and McCallie Avenue, a freestanding dining hall just south of the school building, a new gymnasium on Kyle Street, and a row of dormitories southeast of the school. Opposite page: The steeple of the long-sought chapel did not rise above the campus until 1955.

of thousands of dollars." Since McCallie had become a private, non-profit corporation to facilitate fund raising, the brothers felt it high time for decisive action and volunteered to lead the way. They declared: "We two, 'Professor' and 'Doctor,' are glad to contribute $1,000.00 each to this Greater McCallie (campaign) for we know how badly McCallie needs it."

Better than anyone, the headmasters understood the condition of the school's plant. Campus buildings were cramped, often less than first-rate in construction, and even dangerous at times. The boiler in Douglas Hall threatened to blow once or twice a year, its mounting pressure sounding an alarm that sent students and faculty scurrying outside the dormitory, usually in the dead of winter. Middle Hall had been built solidly in 1906, but the interior walls of North and South halls, added in 1919, were covered in board so flimsy a student could

As they had during the Depression, faculty members (from left) Arthur Lee "Bud" Burns, Chalmers McIlwaine and Wallace Purdy helped steady the school through the years of World War II. Burns received the honorary rank of major from the Board of Trustees so he could serve as interim and, then, assistant commandant, becoming known as "Maj" ever after.

punch a hole in it. Dormitory space was in such short supply that the school had purchased a three-story Victorian-style house on McCallie Avenue on the edge of campus in 1938 to provide room for boarders and classes for the junior school. And fire was a constant threat. Besides the 1907 blaze that destroyed the original frame school building, fire had gutted the attic floor of Founder's Home in 1929. Jarnagin Hall, the dormitory on McCallie Avenue, would burn in a three-alarm blaze in 1952. Fortunately, none of the fires resulted in death or serious injury.

The board took the headmasters' appeal to heart, formally launching The Greater McCallie Building Campaign in September 1941 under the chairmanship of trustee Llewellyn Chapman '21. Its timing, however, was unfortunate. Europe was embroiled in war that began in September 1939 when Germany invaded Poland. While attempting to remain neutral, America was bracing for a widening conflict. School commandant Capt. Herbert Dunlap was called to active duty the same month the headmasters read their letter to the Board. When the Japanese attacked Pearl Harbor in December 1941, America was instantly thrust into the Second World War. More than 1,500 McCallie alumni would serve in all branches of the military from 1941 through 1945.

The public devoured newspaper and newsreel accounts of the fortunes of battle and aided the war effort by planting victory gardens and rationing supplies, from sugar to gasoline. Against this backdrop, the school's fund-raising campaign began. Unable to wait for contributions to build the urgently needed dining facility and add classroom space, the Board voted in December 1941 to borrow $52,000 for construction of Alumni Hall. Ground was broken four days after Pearl Harbor, and the building was completed in 1942 in the midst of a shortage of skilled labor. It would be 1944 before the campaign would generate enough capital to repay the loan.

School enrollment continued to climb, from 358 in 1942 to 419 by 1946, but a new gymnasium and chapel, as well as more dormitory space, would have to await the end of war and the emergence of peacetime prosperity. Still the gift of Alumni Hall represented hard-won dollars at a time when a sizable portion of the donor base was fighting for the country. Robert McCallie and Chalmers

McCallie Commandant Herbert Dunlap (arms folded) returned to the school as a colonel after commanding a regiment in Okinawa in World War II. At right, the Class of 1942 presented the school a plaque memorializing 10 classmates who died serving in four branches of the military during the war.

IN MEMORIAM

The Class of 1942 — which of all McCallie classes suffered the greatest loss of life in World War II — dedicates this memorial in proud tribute to its ten classmates who gave their lives for their country.

US ARMY AIR FORCE
James Arthur Bacon
Edwin Screven Frierson
J. Montgomery Schneider, Jr.
Louis Gray Young
William Durham West, Jr.

US ARMY
Lauren Allen Gates, Jr.
Ben Bob Ross
Charles Sumpter Wylie
US MARINE CORPS
Ruford Patterson Covington

US NAVY
Lemuel Woodward Harrison

"Death is swallowed up in victory." 1 Cor. 15:54

Presented on the occasion of the 50th reunion of the Class of 1942

October 31, 1992

McIlwaine took leading roles in the campaign in its latter years, traveling thousands of miles each summer to solicit gifts. By the time it ended in 1949 with the Homecoming Day dedication of Davenport Memorial Gymnasium in memory of Rodolph Davenport '22 , the Greater McCallie Building Campaign had raised $383,000 and represented McCallie's first sustained fund-raising drive.

With the outbreak of war, military at McCallie changed from mastering the intricacies of close-order drill to learning a pragmatic set of wartime skills: rifle marksmanship, map reading, first aid, scouting and patrolling. Cadets practiced field maneuvers in a wooded lot across McCallie Avenue where poison ivy and chiggers were their biggest foes. At one point, the battalion was enlisted in the search for a German prisoner-of-war who had escaped confinement at the military post in nearby Fort Oglethorpe, GA and was thought hiding on Missionary Ridge. To the relief of those who feared an encounter with a desperate POW, the manhunt proved futile.

With Dunlap's departure, the role of school commandant fell in the war's early years to Arthur Burns. The Board of Trustees conferred on the French teacher and master of dormitories the rank of captain and later major. The man known as "Bud" during his first 17 years at McCallie became "Maj" to students during his final 30 years of service, most boys unaware the title was honorary. When retired Lt. Col. Dana Allen assumed the commandant post in fall 1943, Burns served as his executive officer. Allen relinquished his position when Dunlap returned to McCallie in May 1946 with the rank of colonel. Dunlap's final command was of a regiment in Okinawa where the last contingent of Japanese soldiers hidden in caves surrendered to his forces.

Professor Spencer McCallie, who was named Chattanooga Kiwanis Club Man of the Year in 1943 and Chattanooga's Most Valuable Citizen in 1944 (Park received both honors in 1948), was invaluable to his own students as a member of the local draft board. In that capacity he helped hundreds of McCallie alumni decide in which branch of the armed services to enlist. Six hundred joined the Army, 450 the Navy, 350 the Air Corps and 100 the Marines, Coast Guard and Merchant Marines. McCallie men, who a few short years before had been prying chewing gum from school building floors to work off "marks," were flying bombing sorties as pilots of B-29's.

Amid the rationing of war, the McCallie property seemed not that far removed from its rural past. With gas in short supply, two mules, Tige and Maud, were harnessed to manage the 40-acre campus, hauling garbage and pulling large mowing equipment. Push mowers, hand clippers and sickles were used by groundskeeper Laurence Potts and his son, Carl, to cut the grass and trim the hedges. Still standing was the McCallie homeplace barn, and a small stand of corn grew beside it. A garden supplied other vegetables for the dining hall.

"This was a noisy campus," recalls Spencer McCallie III, who was five years old in 1941. "There was only one tunnel through the Ridge, and trucks would back-fire as they geared down coming through it." The Missionary Ridge streetcar, its wheels screeching against the rails, still wound through campus before crossing McCallie Avenue and climbing Shallowford Road to the crest of the Ridge. The streetcar was the only one in Chattanooga required to carry sand year-round. As a prank, McCallie boys would grease the rails with a cake of soap, and the conductor had to dump sand to gain enough traction to negotiate even a gentle grade.

McCallie depended on the same core of veteran administrators and teachers to guide the school through the upheaval of World War II as had done so through the difficult years of the Depression. Park and Spencer had passed 35 years as co-headmasters when Pearl Harbor was attacked. Associate Headmaster T.E.P. Woods was in his 20th year of meticulously overseeing daily school affairs. C.M.S. McIlwaine, whose indefatigable work ranged from math instructor to athletic director to executive secretary of the Greater McCallie campaign; Wallace Purdy, head of the science department, whose eccentric teaching methods in physics and chemistry classes kept boys attentive and learning; and Arthur Burns, the boarding students' father figure, who could hold up a

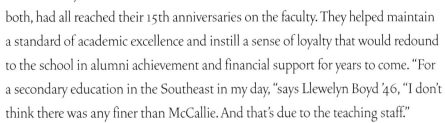

As it was for this 1947 physics class, Saturday "backwork" was the bane of students from the school's earliest days. McCallie's insistence on the mastery of subjects, though, prepared boys well for the academic rigors of college and earned the school a strong reputation in circles of higher education.

hand for five marks of detention or clasp a homesick boy to his chest and be loved for both, had all reached their 15th anniversaries on the faculty. They helped maintain a standard of academic excellence and instill a sense of loyalty that would redound to the school in alumni achievement and financial support for years to come. "For a secondary education in the Southeast in my day, "says Llewelyn Boyd '46, "I don't think there was any finer than McCallie. And that's due to the teaching staff."

With tuition barely covering operating expenses, with bank loans to retire and with no endowment or sustaining fund to help, there was little left to pay teachers, and their salaries were low. An example of the frugality of the time occurred when Russell Tate approached Dr. Park for a raise to help with the expense of a soon-to-be-born second child. "Doctor wheeled around in his chair," recalled Tate, "and looked out the window and ran that crooked finger of his through his hair, and he said, 'Well, Russ, I'm going to tell you something; I didn't have a thing to do with this child coming on. Nothing. But I'll check up and see what we can do about it.'" When new contracts arrived, Tate received a $5 a month raise and was pleased to get it.

Nevertheless, McCallie attracted excellent teachers such as Bill Pressly. A Georgia native and the son of a Presbyterian minister, Pressly had graduated from Princeton with honors in 1931. For a time he wrote advertising copy for The National Broadcasting Corporation from a third-floor office in Rockefeller Center overlooking the famed fountain and skating rink in the heart of Manhattan. But teaching was Pressly's calling, and he answered it in 1936 by applying to McCallie and returning to the South. He was appointed chairman of the school's English Department and given an apartment in Founder's Home.

Pressly found McCallie's prep-school culture fascinating. "I was surprised at how much fun it was to go to faculty meetings," he recalled years later. "We felt quite free to discuss anything we wanted about education." Life in the dorm, he said, exposed him to the "questions and attitudes and confessions" of young men. Pressly observed Park McCallie's "marvelous influence teaching Bible to seniors" and Spencer's "charm and keen thinking. Everyone was crazy about Professor," he said. And Pressly enjoyed describing how McCallie could rattle a brand new teacher, even a minister's son. Doctor Park called on Pressly without warning one evening to give the blessing before the boarding students' meal in South Hall. "I jumped up scared to death and recited the Lord's Prayer," said Pressly, recalling his inept response. "I was halfway through it before I realized what I was doing."

Pressly gained his bearings soon enough. He created the school's required summer reading program, which served up such tomes as *Les Miseables*, *Anna Karenina* and *Moby Dick* when most boys' summer-vacation literary diet consisted of comics. He stocked multiple copies of novels in his classroom so enough were available for every student to participate in class discussion. His stated goals were to teach seniors to read with insight and discrimination and write with accuracy and clarity. He became not only a stellar fixture of the faculty for 15 years but a member of the McCallie family when he married Spencer's daughter, Alice, in 1940. After earning a master's degree in literature from Harvard the following year, Pressly resumed his McCallie career.

✦✦✦

For America, 1945 was a year of jubilation. Germany surrendered in May, ending bombing and bloodshed in Europe, and the Japanese surrendered in September, ending the war. From across the Atlantic and the Pacific, GI's streamed home, grateful for the opportunity to resume civilian life. McCallie celebrated the safe return of alumni who served in the armed forces and honored 62 former students who died in World War II by recording their names on a roll of honor that hung for many years on the second floor of Middle Hall.

At the same time, the school welcomed students to a new fall term that marked the beginning of its fifth decade. In observance of the milestone, nine men sat on the stage of North Hall facing the student body at its first assembly in September 1945. Six of them had been students when the school initially opened its doors in 1905. The others were members of the original faculty: "Doctor," "Professor" and their brother, Ed, the school's first football coach.

For all the look of stability, McCallie was bowing to the winds of change. In August, a month before school began, Spencer had turned 70 and decided it was time to resign as headmaster, dissolving the 40-year partnership with his brother. "Now at the Biblical limit of seventy, I feel as if I ought to give up the title and the honors to the younger men of the school," he explained in a letter to alumni. T.E.P. Woods also turned 70 in June 1945, and he, too, resigned.

Park would serve as sole headmaster with the help of three associate headmasters: his son, Bob '29, English instructor and director of athletics and soon-to-be chief fundraiser; his nephew, Spencer (Spence), Jr. '28, principal of the Junior School and director of admissions; and Spencer, Sr.'s son-in-law, Bill Pressly, head of the English Department and director of scholarship. Spencer, Sr. noted he would continue to serve as president of the McCallie Board of Trustees and teach his popular Old Testament class to Junior School students. "No one would notice any difference," he assured alumni, "save the titles in the catalogue."

In fact, the school was in the midst of its first major transition in leadership. Park McCallie would follow his brother's example by resigning as headmaster upon his 70th birthday in August 1949. This dramatic change was cushioned by the emergence of a second generation of McCallies to follow in the brothers' footsteps and further eased by the steadying presence of Burns, McIlwaine, Dunlap and Purdy, four key department heads who had served the school since 1925. While the retirement of founding headmasters threw some schools into turmoil, McCallie maintained its continuity of mission.

In May 1947, before Park retired as headmaster and while Spencer was still walking with brisk, long strides from his home at 16 Shallowford Road to the school each day to teach Bible, more than 400 alumni and friends gathered for a surprise testimonial dinner for the two men in the ballroom of the Read House hotel. If the honorees were stunned by the lavish occasion, attendees were amazed by a reversal of roles. Known for a sparkling wit that delighted audiences for decades, Spencer was uncharacteristically serious in his remarks. The devout Park, on the other hand, regaled the crowd with a whimsical, irreverent sense of humor. When his time came to speak, he said the banquet came as such a surprise that he momentarily thought he had "laid aside my mortal coils" and gone to heaven. But, he noted, upon looking at those assembled and seeing some he thought would never enter the pearly gates, he had promptly changed his mind.

Featured speaker Dr. Francis Gaines, president of Washington and Lee University, praised the

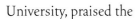

Davenport Memorial Gymnasium was dedicated in 1949 in memory of Rodolph Davenport '22. Like Alumni Hall, dedicated in 1942, the gym was the result of the school's first significant fund-raising drive, The Greater McCallie Building Campaign. The gymnasium was later incorporated in the Sports and Activity Center.

two for their contribution to education in the South, and alumni presented them with two leatherbound albums filled with more than 800 letters of appreciation. It was a fitting and timely tribute to more than 40 years of devoted effort by each. Spencer, Jr. would later say the two brothers had no idea of the magnitude of the task they would shoulder when their father, the Rev. McCallie, agreed to provide them the land and buildings to start the school. Bill Pressly found it amazing that their appetite for the work at hand never flagged. "They were remarkable men," he said, "in that they were just as active at the end of their careers as at the beginning."

Park's retirement as headmaster in 1949 raised the delicate issue of succession. Spencer, Jr., Bob and Bill Pressly had since 1945 served as associate headmasters under Park. At a meeting in February 1949 at Lockett Lodge, the McCallie Board's Search Committee cited an "embarrassment of talent" in trying to choose among the three and, "based upon the peculiar facts which exist

From 1949 to 1951, McCallie was directed by a unique, three-person Board of Headmasters comprised of, at bottom from left, William Pressly, Spencer McCallie, Jr. and Robert McCallie. The McCallie cousins became co-headmasters in 1951 when Pressly accepted the presidency of Atlanta's Westminster Schools. Below: The 1947 faculty gathers on the steps of Alumni Hall.

in this school," made an unusual recommendation. The committee proposed that each of the men be designated "headmaster," equal in rank and pay. Together, they would comprise a McCallie School Board of Headmasters, and they would rotate as chairman. Trustees unanimously approved the unique proposal and named Bill Pressly as the first chairman.

While the school's leadership was being decided, a campus drama was unfolding. In the spring of 1949, Spencer was diagnosed with incurable acute leukemia. Though facing a terminal illness, he continued to serve as president of the Board of Trustees and began another term of teaching seventh-grade Bible in fall 1949, with grandson Spencer III among the students in his class.

Professor Spencer McCallie taught his popular, seventh-grade Old Testament Bible Class until a week before his death in October 1949. Among his final fall-semester students were seven sons of McCallie alumni, including his grandson, Spencer III, seated at his right, who would become the school's headmaster 25 years later.

Men who drove him to the hospital every ten days for life-extending transfusions were amazed at his zest for living and equanimity in facing death, even joking about his demise. On October 18, 1949, several days after teaching his last class, the man who had animated the campus from its founding succumbed to the disease at the age of 74.

Mourning his loss, Alfred Mynders, editor of *The Chattanooga Times*, wrote of the energy Spencer brought to civic endeavors. "He often came to the rescue of lagging causes, to spur tired educators to fresh efforts on behalf of Southern youth, and, with laughter as his weapon," wrote Mynders, "he could stop failure dead in its tracks." Former student Brainerd Cooper '21, editor of the *Chattanooga News-Free Press*, eulogized Spencer as one who "understood and loved boys, and they understood and loved him." Of his cheerfulness to the end, Cooper wrote: "He died with the calm and willingness of Socrates, but with a buoyancy of spirit that was Spencer McCallie."

America's post-war optimism and prosperity could not have emerged at a better time for the school. As 1950 arrived, McCallie found itself in a familiar predicament: too little campus for too many students. The Greater McCallie Building Campaign of the '40s had addressed two urgent needs: a freestanding dining hall and the new Davenport Gymnasium. But with enrollment straining against a cap of 425 students, the school was still wrestling with inadequate facilities. The aging academic building lacked six general classrooms, as well as 20 seats in the library and 70 seats in study hall, to accommodate the student population. Even more pressing was the absence of modern dormitory space. Boys were scattered in ten buildings – four of them off campus, some of them makeshift and none of them fireproof.

Counting on the support of more than 3,500 living alumni, the Board of Trustees authorized the McCallie Fiftieth Anniversary Campaign in 1950, with an unprecedented goal of raising $1 million by the school's 50th anniversary in 1955. Chaired by Jack Whitaker '23, the ambitious capital campaign to revitalize the campus chose as its first project the construction of a brick, fireproof dorm to house 102 boys. Built on the site of the McCallie homeplace barn and garden,

McCallie's campus stayed active throughout the year. A highly successful summer camp that offered sports, crafts, camp-outs and the lake acquainted prospective students with the campus and faculty and provided revenue for the school. At the same time, summer school courses were held in the academic building.

Hutcheson Hall, named for patron John L. Hutcheson, founder of Peerless Woolen Mills and father of alumni John, Jr. and Lewis, was dedicated in June 1951. Dr. Clarence Wilcox, who had remained a steadfast friend of McCallie since leaving it 30 years earlier to become president of Darlington School in Rome, GA, gave the dedicatory address.

By the end of 1952, the campaign had raised $650,000 toward its $1 million goal. Those funds had also enabled the school to remodel Douglas Hall and install sprinkler systems in both Douglas and Founder's Home. The school was removing the constant threat of fires. Shortly after Hutcheson was dedicated, the Board of Trustees authorized construction of a second, smaller dormitory. Dedicated in October 1953 in honor of patron Robert J. Maclellan, founder of Provident Insurance Company and father of alumni Robert L. and Hugh O. Maclellan, Maclellan Hall housed 40 boys just east of the academic building.

As the anniversary campaign continued toward its goal, the Board, at a September 1953 meeting, approved a project that would fulfill Park McCallie's cherished dream. Work began the following spring on a $380,000 chapel that would serve as both the religious and cultural center of the school. Able to seat 625 people in pews, the brick building rose from the north end of campus as a sign of the school's faith-centered program. In December 1954, Park watched along with two dozen cadets as a crane with an extended boom placed the 50-foot frame steeple atop the 85-foot-high masonry tower that was decked with four clocks. The centerpiece of the million-dollar campaign, the chapel would be dedicated in May 1955 as part of the school's 50th anniversary celebration.

At his first day of school at McCallie in fall 1954, 12-year-old Harry Whitney Durand III drew unwanted attention. With the chapel under construction and assemblies still held in North Hall study hall, the seventh-grader was called to the stage to be introduced to the student body as the school's first third-generation student. His father, Harry W. Durand, Jr., graduated in 1928, and his grandfather, Harry W. Durand, Sr. had attended for one year, in 1907. A milestone event for the school was a mortifying experience for young Durand, who could see the snicker of older students as his family's McCallie history was recited. "When you're that young, to be placed before nearly 500 students, many of whom were laughing, is intimidating," he recalls. "The senior and sophomore between whom I was seated in study hall never let me forget it. They called me '3' from then on."

Dr. Park McCallie proudly registers the school's first third-generation student, Harry Whitney Durand III, in the fall of 1954, as his father, Harry, Jr. '28, and grandfather, Harry, Sr. '07, look on. McCallie approached its 50th anniversary with a growing and supportive base of alumni.

But McCallie was rightfully proud of having educated three generations of youth and of the mark they were making in the world. Graduates of notable public achievement ranged from Rhyne Killian '21, president of Massachusetts Institute of Technology, to crusading *Atlanta Constitution* editorialist Ralph McGill '17, a principal architect of the New South vision of racial progress and business development. Senator and ambassador Howard Baker '43 and media mogul Ted Turner '56 maintained that tradition.

Another hallmark of the school lay in the passing of its top administrative post from two brothers to their two sons. Spencer McCallie, Jr. and his first cousin, Robert, had begun serving with Spencer's brother-in-law, Bill Pressly, as a unique, three-person board of headmasters in 1949. But in the summer of 1951, Pressly resigned from McCallie to accept the founding presidency of the Westminster Schools in Atlanta. "Everything I was doing, Bob and Spence could do," said Pressly of his decision to leave and accept the challenge of starting a new school. Of McCallie's unusual experiment in prep-school administration, he declared, "A triumverate isn't supposed to work, but it worked beautifully."

Spence and Bob were now alone to follow in their fathers' footsteps. Though of contrasting natures, they complemented each other as Professor and Doctor had done before them. Cerebral and mild-mannered, Bob, who taught advanced senior English, spoke with a scholar's locution, which didn't spare him the occasional gaffe. Once, he encouraged cadets considering attending an out-of-town game to use seats available on GPS buses to "increase the population," a notion that was greeted with a roar of approval. Another time, he inadvertently stepped into the line of fire as one boy sprang from behind a door to spit a mouthful of water at another and waved off the mishap without punishing either.

Spence, on the other hand, was the school's plain-spoken voice of rectitude. His sense of indignation could quell mischief, be it a solitary offense or a senior-class prank. Like his father, he served as advisor to the Student Senate and had the unpleasant task of informing parents when their sons were being punished or expelled. Spence, though, could join Bob in lighter moments. During one assembly, Bob asked students to refrain from referring to Spence behind his back by the nickname, "Monk," as it hurt Spence's feelings. That was Spence's prearranged cue to swing across the stage on a rope and disappear before the disbelieving eyes of the student body.

The co-headmasters' path was made easier by relying on the seasoned experience of McIlwaine, Burns, Purdy and Dunlap. Members of the quartet that came to McCallie in 1925 were named associate headmasters in 1952. Meanwhile, energetic new teachers and coaches, many of whom would spend their careers at McCallie, were invigorating the faculty in the early

The dedication of the McCallie Chapel in May 1955 was a testament to the school's faith-centered emphasis and fund-raising prowess. Maclellan Hall, at the top, dedicated in 1953, and Hutcheson Hall, not pictured, dedicated in 1951, were other facilities made possible by the school's million-dollar Fiftieth Anniversary Campaign.

1950's. They included Warren James, John Day, Patrick McKinsey, W.O.E.A. Humphries, Harold Echart, Harry Milligan, John Pataky, James Ware and Ed Lundien. They joined Russell Tate, Thomas and Mary Walker, Dave Spencer, Houston Patterson, Elliott Schmidt and John Strang, who had arrived in the 1940's, the latter inheriting Professor McCallie's Bible class in 1949. Dr. James Bibb, who had served as school physician from 1913 until his death in 1952, was succeeded by Dr. David McCallie, Professor McCallie's youngest son.

McCallie teachers and coaches displayed a professionalism and dedication that kept the school successful in the classroom and on the field. In athletics, the school claimed Mid-South Association championships in football, baseball and track in 1947-48 and was recognized in 1949 as the only Mid-South member school to field a team in every association-sanctioned sport for the past 15 years.

The 1951 football team was Mid-South champion with an 8-0-1 record, and the 1954-55 school year saw McCallie win Mid-South crowns in four sports: football, wrestling, cross-country and track. Owing in part to a steep home course called Billy Goat Hill that ran midway up Missionary Ridge and left opponents wobbly with exhaustion, McCallie dominated cross-country in the region, sweeping the first six titles after the sport was introduced in Mid-South competition. In 1956, Russell Tate, the longtime dean of the Junior School, became only the third Mid-South coach to win championships in three different sports (basketball, track and cross-country). The other coaches to achieve the feat were also from McCallie: Dave Spencer (wrestling, baseball and football) and Kenneth "Bitsy" Howard (football, basketball and baseball).

At the same time, McCallie burnished its reputation as one of the top college preparatory schools in the South. In the 1950's, the school began offering accelerated classes in English, math and science and established a chapter of Cum Laude to recognize the school's top performing students. McCallie seniors attended leading public and private universities in the region — Vanderbilt and Emory, North Carolina and Virginia — as well as Ivy League schools. In 1957, McCallie graduates had the highest freshman average at Vanderbilt University. The following year, McCallie had more Merit Semifinalists than any other school in the South.

As enrollment nudged upward to 500 students, more academic space was needed. On the heels of the $1 million Fiftieth Anniversary Campaign, the Board authorized another fund-raising drive to collect a third of a million dollars for a separate Junior School building and a freestanding indoor pool. Attached to the south end of the main school structure, the three-story Junior

School was dedicated in 1958. The following year, the Goree Nelson Memorial Pool was dedicated in memory of Robert Goree Nelson, Jr. '39, who died serving in the Naval Air Force in World War II.

The period from 1949 to 1959 represented the greatest decade of construction in McCallie history to that time and validated the founders' wisdom in converting the school to a non-profit organization. The private Board of Trustees, which had celebrated its 20th anniversary in 1957, had managed to raise $2 million in contributions since 1937 and transform the campus. "The school's success depended on the faith of those people," David McCallie says of the early trustees. "They believed what Father and Uncle Park were trying to do, and they bit into it. They led a knock-on-the-doors and letter-writing campaign, buttonholing people who believed in McCallie to get them to give. They took on the school as a cause, and it has grown from there."

In 1960, McCallie seemed a bastion of stability. Though Purdy had left the faculty in 1956 to work for the Atomic Energy Commission's isotope program at

--- ◆◆◆ ---

Mac Patton sinks a shot against Baylor in 1953 and Pat Liles wins the 100-yard dash at the Baylor Relays in 1955 as McCallie competed with Baylor through the '40s, '50s and '60s in every sport except football. The 1960 McCallie football team compiled an 8-1-0 record and earned students a rare holiday by defeating the state's top-ranked team, Bradley County, ending its 21-game winning streak.

--- ◆◆◆ ---

Oak Ridge, TN and Dunlap had retired as commandant in 1959, to be succeeded by Col. DeVere Armstrong, a solid nucleus of teachers remained, and the patterned flow of activity — of daily classes and sports and drill — continued. Like his father, Whitney Durand graduated as regimental major in 1960. Like his father, Spencer McCallie, Jr. was preparing to head the Southern Association of Colleges and Secondary Schools. Like his grandfather and father, Park and Bob McCallie, Jim McCallie had come to the school to teach. As they had in the past, the Board contemplated another major building campaign.

But the next two decades would shake McCallie to its foundation. The culture was changing, as the war in Vietnam bred a strong anti-military, anti-authoritarian sentiment. The demographic was shifting; the baby boom was passing through high school into college and enrollments were shrinking. The competition was stiffening; preparatory day schools were opening all at once in Charlotte, Atlanta, Birmingham, Nashville and Winston-Salem — cities that had supplied a steady stream of McCallie boarders for years.

"The world was changing under us," says Spencer McCallie III of those tumultuous years, "and we didn't know what was going on." It would take the courage of radical decisions and the bedrock strength of the school to make the passage that lay ahead.

The school had a uniform for different seasons and occasions and required students to be in it whenever in public. Modeling combinations of military dress in 1957 were, from left, Fred Wunderlich, David Hickey, Franklin McCallie, Jerry Crouch, John Tessman and Marshall McCallie.

Making the Passage

1961-1980

O N AN AUGUST SUNDAY AFTERNOON IN 1961, seventy-five McCallie faculty members and their spouses stood inside the departure gate of Lovell Field to wish a joyful bon voyage to Arthur Lee and Millie Burns. The dean of students and his wife were boarding an Eastern Airlines flight from Chattanooga to New York City, where they would set sail on the Queen Elizabeth for Europe and a three-week, all-expense-paid vacation to Paris and London. The Class of '61 had planned the surprise trip as an affectionate tribute to Burns for more than 35 years of service to the school, and they had enlisted the willing support of parents, students and alumni to cover expenses. Dressed in a dark suit with a trench coat draped over one arm, the dean stood with his wife on the stairway ramp of the plane and waved to the cheering crowd below them, his characteristically taciturn countenance wreathed in a rare, broad smile.

Unbeknownst to those attending the airport sendoff, McCallie would soon be bidding farewell to elements of its traditional past. The military trappings that had been woven into McCallie life since World War I would vanish in 10 years. The generation of schoolmen that Burns represented would all depart the faculty in the next dozen years. The aging academic building would disappear in 15. The authoritarian discipline that had been a cornerstone of the school for nearly 60 years would clash with a culture of protest and permissiveness. Yet, when the dust settled on two decades of contentious change, the school would more than survive. It would embark on a bold, new trajectory.

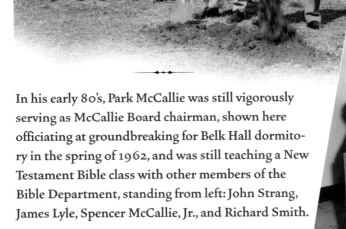

In his early 80's, Park McCallie was still vigorously serving as McCallie Board chairman, shown here officiating at groundbreaking for Belk Hall dormitory in the spring of 1962, and was still teaching a New Testament Bible class with other members of the Bible Department, standing from left: John Strang, James Lyle, Spencer McCallie, Jr., and Richard Smith.

Tradition was in full bloom as the 1960's arrived. Spencer (Dr. Spence) McCallie, Jr. and his first cousin, Robert (Dr. Bob) McCallie, were the school's second-generation co-headmasters. Robert McCallie's father, Park, the school's co-founder, was serving as chairman of the Board of Trustees and still teaching a New Testament Bible class at the ripe age of 80. Three stalwarts of the faculty, who had begun teaching in 1925 — Chalmers McIlwaine, Herbert Dunlap and Burns – were serving (in Dunlap's case, would return shortly to serve) as associate headmasters. And the next generation of the McCallie family was entering the fold. Jim McCallie, Dr. Bob's son, had joined the faculty in 1961. Dr. Spence's son, Spencer III, would arrive two years later.

The school launched another of what had become a continuous series of capital campaigns to modernize the physical plant. In 1961, the Capital Gifts Program for the Sixties set a million-dollar goal to eliminate all substandard dormitory rooms on campus. North and South Hutcheson Halls and Maclellan Hall had been built in the early 1950's to begin replacing dorms that were holdovers from the school's early days. The new campaign, chaired by Hugh Huffaker, Jr. '48, sought to complete the process. Though the campaign surpassed a million dollars in gifts and pledges in three years instead of the allotted five, construction couldn't wait. As in the past, the school borrowed money to get needed projects underway immediately.

Vigorously flinging a shovel full of dirt to the amusement of onlookers, a spry Park McCallie broke ground in early 1962 for Belk Hall, the school's new senior dorm. It opened that fall and was dedicated the following spring in honor of the family of the late William Henry Belk of Charlotte, NC, founder of Belk Store Enterprises, who had sent four sons to McCallie. At the same time, work was proceeding on a new front for Founder's Home that would add student rooms and faculty apartments and replace the original Victorian facade with ornate Corinthian columns. When these projects were completed, the school could boast of an "outstanding dormitory plant, which should prove completely adequate for years to come."

As soon as the Founder's Home and Belk Hall work was finished, the school razed Douglas Hall and constructed on its site a brick, Colonial-style administration building. Dedicated in May 1964 in honor of school trustee Hardwick Caldwell, Sr. and his sons, the new building freed space for eight more classrooms and the enlargement of the library and laboratories in North, Middle and South Halls, breathing a few more years of life into an academic building that was groaning with age.

Vestiges of the courtly South were apparent in the uniforms, gowns and cotillion-like pageantry of the school's formal dances. The Officer's Ball (above) culminated in a procession underneath an arch of drawn sabers. The military gave boys a chance to visibly wear their accomplishments, in braid on their shoulders and bars on their chest.

McCallie's multi-generational leadership: At left, co-headmaster Robert McCallie and his son, Jim, flank Robert's father, co-founder Park McCallie. Behind them is a portrait of Park's father, Rev. Thomas H. McCallie. At right, future headmaster Spencer McCallie III stands behind his father, headmaster Spencer McCallie, Jr. Behind them is school co-founder Spencer McCallie, Sr.

For a moment in the early 1960's, McCallie, like the rest of America, rested between two worlds: the calm and stability of the post World War II period and the foment that would be unleashed by the Civil Rights movement and the Vietnam War. Whitlow Wallace, who graduated in 1963, recalled the highly regimented student life that still defined the McCallie of his day. "You were expected to be a scholar in the classroom, an athlete on the field, a sharp cadet in the military and a gentleman at all times," he says. "It was a tough road."

The military at McCallie would be one of the first casualties of changes sweeping society that would give the school a different cast. With the country's slide into war in Vietnam and the rising tide of American casualties it produced, a sharp generational divide on attitude toward the military emerged. In 1967, after Col. John J. Moore succeeded Col. Devere Armstrong as the school's professor of military science, the school conducted a poll to measure feelings within the McCallie community toward continuation of military training. By 53-47, the school's seniors voted to abandon the program. Their parents voted 57-6 to retain it.

Through the latter part of the 1960's, arguments for dropping military at McCallie grew stronger. The majority of top-ranked prep schools in the country didn't offer military training. Meanwhile, boarding schools with a military component suffered from the perception that they were academic boot camps for the problem children of affluent families. Even the most prestigious military academies, such as Culver in Indiana where Park began his teaching career, were failing to attract enough qualified students. Finally, drill was taking a valuable class period each day as well as nightly preparation time from academics. As David McCallie, the school's physician at the time, notes: "Boys were shining their belt buckles and shoes when college entrance requirements were rising."

Finally, in the spring of 1970, the Board voted to drop

McCallie began broadening its offering in the arts in the mid-1960's and maintained its traditional competitiveness in sports. The 1965-66 soccer team won the Mid-South championship. The 1970 cross-country team takes the measure of St. Andrews on the home course's infamous Billy Goat Hill.

all military training by the end of the academic year. The formal announcement came at the Mother's Day Parade in May. Students reacted with "joy and triumph," the *Pennant* declared. Reaction from alumni and faculty was mixed. Some felt the discipline, leadership experience and sense of accomplishment that military training offered would be an irreparable loss. (Curiously, some of McCallie's most successful alumni through the years had

been "senior privates" who marched to their own cadence.) Others questioned the program's practical value in the first place. Bill Pressly, who served as headmaster with Spence and Bob in the early 1950's, observed that McCallie gradu-

ates who entered Georgia Tech were exempt from only one quarter of college ROTC training. "If what you did five times a week for five years could be done in one quarter, it seemed to me to be a waste of time," he said.

Many alumni were ambivalent. They accepted the need for more course credits yet clung to stirring memories of the drum roll preceding The Star Spangled Banner, the Dunlap Rifles' execution of intricate maneuvers without a spoken command and the pageantry of full-dress parades. "We had this wonderful color guard that carried all the flags of the Southeastern states with the American flag in front," recalls Spencer McCallie III, fondly. "It was impressive."

Fortunately, scholastics and character development had always been far more important than military training at McCallie and that emphasis assured the school's survival. Many essentially military schools, where cadets marched to meals, saluted officers during the day, lived in barracks and faced the rigors of white-glove inspections but not the demands of a highly challenging academic curriculum, were forced to close when anti-military sentiment swept the country and their enrollments plunged. In the fall of 1971, McCallie returned to where it began in the fall of 1905, with boys attending school in ties and blazers.

From 1965, when Robert McCallie died, until 1974, Spencer McCallie, Jr. was the school's sole headmaster. He dealt with changing student behavior by combining a hard-line approach to discipline with a prickly sense of humor. A student kite-flying foray to Chickamauga Battlefield, at left, drew the aging headmaster's enjoyment of boyish exuberance.

The McCallie School
Missionary Ridge
Chattanooga, Tennessee

August 1965

Dear Patron and Student:

The McCallie School does not look with favor on the present tendency of too many boys having effeminate locks. We expect our boys to return to school with a reasonable haircut, and our idea of what is reasonable might differ with some of our students. We suggest to them that we are on the conservative side. As best I can spell it out, side burns should not be longer than to be even with the corners of the eyes; sides of head light to medium; hair on top of head no longer than three inches, and not down over the forehead; neck clipped to even with bottom of lobe of ear and rather tapered. Any boy coming to school with hair that jolts our rather dogmatic idea will be required to get a haircut at once and will also be placed on campus for two weeks. Neither do we plan to fight this problem all year.

We suggest that if a boy feels that he is going to be miserable without long hair, that if he needs a beauty parlor rather than a barber shop, it could well be he is making a mistake in coming here. We do not like to be so arbitrary with reference to one's personal grooming, but to be very frank, we just can't take the "beetle look."

Sincerely,

Spencer McCallie
Headmaster

American society was also confronting the issue of integration. In 1966, 28 McCallie faculty members, including the two headmasters' sons, Jim and Spencer III, signed a petition calling on the school to adopt an open-admissions policy, accepting students of any race. The Board delayed action, adopting a wait-and-see approach to the volatile issue until March 1969, when trustees voted in favor of day-school integration, and January 1970, when they approved the integration of the boarding school as well.

The first African-American graduate of McCallie, David Chatman '75 of Louisville, KY, entered as a sophomore in 1972. By his senior year, he had been inducted into Keo-Kio, been elected to the Student Council, lettered in three varsity sports and been accepted to Vanderbilt University. The door to minorities was now open but, as with other Southern private schools, McCallie made slow progress at first in diversifying its student body. The pace quickened in the 1980's when the national ABC (A Better Chance) program, which provided financial aid to place promising minority students in excellent secondary schools, brought highly qualified applicants to McCallie.

Since the early 1960's, the school's regional reputation and a large "baby boom" pool of applicants had kept the number of boarding admissions to McCallie high. But by the early 1970's, the boom was beginning to slacken while, at the same time, private day schools were opening in major Southern cities, capturing students whose families traditionally sent them to McCallie for a first-rate education. This combination of events — not to mention a deteriorating academic building that was beginning to scare prospects away — caught the school unprepared.

As the 1970's arrived, the school's old guard was departing. At right, Herbert Dunlap and Arthur Lee Burns were honored at a banquet in August 1972 upon their retirement after 42 and 47 years respectively on the faculty. At left, Chalmers McIlwaine retired in June 1974 after 49 years of service that ranged from mathematics department chairman to athletics director.

Spencer McCallie III began an energetic and progressive, 25-year tenure as headmaster in 1974 by improving faculty salaries, opening new academic facilities and enlarging the endowment. With traits ranging from the visionary to the storyteller, he guided the school with a relaxed style and strong presence.

When Spencer McCallie III became director of admissions at the start of the 1970's, he needed only six more students to fill out the boarding class that year, and failed to get them. "We weren't watching the demographics," he says in retrospect. "There was little recruiting and no one traveling." Of those boarders who did come to McCallie, too many were being expelled each year for academic or disciplinary reasons. By 1974, admissions to the boarding program had dwindled to half that of the day program. The following year, the school intentionally accepted even fewer boarders in an effort to eliminate high-risk students. Vacancies in the boarding department required that the third floor of South Hutcheson Hall be temporarily closed. There was concern about the future of dorm life at McCallie, but the decision was made to strengthen the student recruitment program and enhance school facilities. Eliminating military was one thing; abandoning the boarding program was a different matter.

The cultural revolution sweeping American campuses in the mid-1970's gave McCallie a different look and feel, as evident in John McCall's Spanish II class in 1974. Despite dramatic changes in hair and dress codes, the school maintained its core values and traditions and its reputation for academic excellence.

The counter-culture movement among American youth that arose in the 1960's with the Vietnam War and continued in its aftermath expressed itself in a number of ways, from anti-authoritarian sentiment to issues of grooming and dress to a growing use of drugs on the nation's high school campuses. McCallie tried various tactics to combat the latter, including raids on dorm rooms that bred mistrust of the faculty. Eventually, the school adopted a second-offense policy with the possibility of re-admission following counseling.

"We didn't do well at first with the drug culture in the '70s," concedes Spencer III. "I learned that there are things bigger than you, that you're not going to change the culture. It was a difficult and humbling time."

Despite the emotional freight of the era, student life at McCallie was still filled with the rules, rituals and commonplace enjoyments of boyhood on the Ridge. "McCallie was such a cocoon," recalls Hal Daughdrill III '73, a boarder from Atlanta. "We were, for the most part, in our own world. We knew a war was going on and the draft existed, but it didn't dominate our conversation." He recalls that Major Burns, like a mother hen, still checked the names of boarding students at breakfast, where, as with all meals, a teacher sat at each table and no one ate until the blessing was said. On weekends, boarders, who depended on local motorists for shuttle transportation, used the "ride line" with pick-up points at McCallie Avenue in front of the chapel and the Krispy Kreme donut shop on Brainerd Road, a location sweetly emblazoned in Daughdrill's mind after many years.

For day students like Rob Huffaker '78, there were still the gentle hazing that accompanied his status as a seventh-grade "pygmy" and the Junior School teachers that ranged from the gruff-sounding John Day to the gentle John Strang. "They instilled confidence in young men," Huffaker says of the faculty. "The moral base of the school was always there." Adds Daughdrill: "McCallie was always intent on turning out boys with great hearts connected to great minds."

Leading the school into these challenging times was an administrative team that had been raised two eras earlier. In 1970, Spencer, Jr. was 61 and looking forward to retirement in four years. The associate headmasters, Burns, McIlwaine and Dunlap, were approaching their 70's. Younger men were in the wings, but the full weight of responsibility fell on aging shoulders.

The difficulty of their task had been compounded by the sudden death of Robert McCallie. Three days before Thanksgiving 1965, as he was leaving the Chattanooga airport after placing his daughter, Margaret Ann, on a plane to visit her brother, Jim, who was working on his master's degree in New York City, Bob McCallie died of a heart attack. It fell to Spencer, Jr. to break the news to his uncle, Park, the octogenarian chairman of the school board, who still came to an office each day at Caldwell Hall.

Even 30 years afterward, Dr. Spence recalled the scene with emotion. "That wonderful man," he said of Dr. Park, "his oldest son ("Parkie") having died when he was just a youth, and then Bob, who meant so much to him and whom he was so proud of — to go in and tell him that Bob had died. I broke down and was crying and couldn't talk. And Uncle Park said, 'Spence, what's the trouble?' I blurted out, more or less, 'Uncle Park, Bob is dead.' He sat there for a moment and then said, 'Bob is dead?' I nodded. And then he said, 'The Lord will sustain.' And from then on, he was a brick. I choke up to think about it or try to tell it."

Robert McCallie's loss to the school was profound. He had been "Mr. Outside," managing business operations and traveling the South each summer in search of alumni gifts for capital campaigns. He also brought a scholarly presence to the faculty, teaching English 5, the advanced literature course for seniors; delivering erudite devotionals at assembly; and addressing the school's public functions. Spencer had lost the partner with whom he divided headmaster's duties and his boyhood friend. For a time, he felt overwhelmed. "I realized I had to pick it all up, get it all together," he said.

With the support of the Board of Trustees, and the special assistance of trustee Mark Wilson, who visited Spencer every day at his office for a time, he did just that. From the end of 1965 until July 1974, when he retired, Spencer served as the school's sole headmaster. In the face of the rebelliousness of the day, he spoke with unmistakable authority. He could both berate and encourage a boy, and he preached the virtues of moral fiber and "deee-zire" both in private conversation and chapel addresses. An old-school moralist, he warned so often of succumbing to "the cheap and shoddy" that the *Pennant* published a picture of sheep in a field and whimsically captioned it: "Sheep in Soddy."

His confrontational style offended some, particularly when he reprimanded the student body en masse, but unlike some headmasters who grew brittle with age, he retained a sense of humor. Once, after badgering boys about their long hair, he appeared at assembly wearing a self-mocking Beatles' wig. When the school created Mapes Day in 1971 as a way to relieve the daily pressure of classes, Spence joined in the kite-flying frivolity at Chickamauga Battlefield. He could match his father's legendary vigor, too. On his 60th birthday, before a hushed assembly, Spence jumped flatfooted from the floor to the stage as he promised he would do, clearing the difficult height by a fraction of an inch. As he stood up from accomplishing the impressive feat, the chapel erupted in applause and cheers.

As the 1970's arrived, with men approaching their 70th birthdays still running the school, a generational change in leadership was at hand. Arthur

Burns and Herbert Dunlap retired in 1972. Chalmers McIlwaine retired with Spencer in 1974. Both Burns and McIlwaine had served McCallie for nearly 50 years each. The men who had led the school since the Depression were gone.

So was co-founder Park McCallie, who died in 1971 at the age of 91. "He was never ordained," eulogized *The Chattanooga Times*, "but he led as active a ministry of service as many a man of the cloth." The man who in 1905 had beseeched his father and prodded his brother to help him start a school to educate Southern youth had seen his dream miraculously fulfilled. Several days before his death, he received visits from captains of the football and wrestling teams and reminisced with his daughter, Anne, about the boys and classes he'd known through the years. At the last, he said wistfully to Anne: "We had a wonderful time, didn't we?"

A rmed with an understanding of the school's most pressing needs and the youthful vigor to address them, 38-year-old Spencer McCallie III '55 followed his father as headmaster in 1974. His rise as a third-generation headmaster, a rarity in the history of American independent secondary education, had been steady. He joined the faculty in 1963 after earning a bachelor's degree in English with honors from Vanderbilt University and serving three years in the Navy. With his wife, Sara, and two daughters, he moved into Founder's Home, where he had been raised. He proceeded to teach English and chair the department, direct the summer school program, earn a master's degree in education with honors from Harvard University, and succeed his cousin Jim as admissions director when Jim left McCallie in 1969 to head The Brookstone School in Columbus, GA. Spencer was named associate headmaster in 1971 and, two years later, headmaster-elect.

His ascendancy following an 11-year apprenticeship was not entirely assured, however. "Older trustees, I was told, had to be convinced I was not too young and radical," Spencer says. "I can understand their concern. I had never served in another school, and my experience was relatively limited." Yet, he had gained additional seasoning as the private-school representative to the State Committee for Accreditation and as a member of the Headmasters' Association, where he met other young Southern heads. And having grown up on campus, he knew McCallie from the inside out. Trustee Bill Spears '24, who served on the committee that picked Spencer III for the job, came away impressed with the man who would take the school's reins. "I think he is the best-balanced young man I've ever known," he declared.

In implementing the decisions to abandon the military and to open the doors to minority students, Spencer's father, Dr. Spence, had led McCallie through some of its most difficult passages. He had also maintained the school's high expectations for academic achievement and personal integrity during years of student unrest. In this gallant effort, he had been assisted by the aging Dunlap, Burns and McIlwaine. While many schools foundered on the rocky shoals of the '60s and '70s, McCallie stayed the course. "If they had not been great schoolmen," says Spencer III of the elderly team of administrators, "they could not have pulled it off."

At the end of his tenure, with Spencer III taking the major role in facility planning at the school and with a galvanized Board of Trustees propelling it, Dr. Spence saw the launch of a campaign to make McCallie "the best preparatory school in the South." Chaired by L. Hardwick Caldwell, Jr. and unveiled in December 1972, the McCallie Development Fund sought an unprecedented $6.35 million for construction of a new academic facility "to replace McCallie's deteriorated and inflexible present structure," as well as to enlarge a paltry endowment.

It would fall to the son to bring the vision to fruition. Spencer III began a 25-year tenure that would see the school financially, physically and academically transformed. Assisting him were Warren James '43 and Houston Patterson

The old academic building, which stood while the new academic center was under construction (page 86), was demolished (at right) in the summer of 1976. Students formed a human chain to move books from the old library stacks to the new. The school quadrangle emerged with the completion and opening (below) of Maclellan Academic Center, Hunter Arts Center and Tate Hall in the fall of 1976.

'43 as associate headmasters; Miles McNiff, a Yale University graduate, as academic dean; George Hazard, Jr. '64 as director of admissions; and Mel Cooper, who would become the school's first fulltime director of development.

The capital campaign inherited by Spencer III was a response to the school's protracted financial problems. McCallie never had a single benefactor who could sustain the school or a professional development program that could build adequate reserves. While alumni had supported a succession of capital campaigns, their gifts rarely funded projects in full, and unlike its competitors, McCallie had no multi-million-dollar endowment to cover the difference. (McCallie's endowment was $300,000 in 1974; Baylor's, at $6 million, was 20 times larger.) Instead, the school continually borrowed money from banks and serviced the debt by siphoning from the operating budget funds that would have otherwise gone to salaries and staffing. As for undertaking a major project like a new academic building, it had long been deferred.

But the school's hand-to-mouth existence was claiming too high a price. George Hazard, who became director of admissions in 1973, once described the impression that the exposed pipes, marked-up walls and wooden floors of the academic building made on prospective students. "They'd look and their mouths would drop, and we'd never see them again," he said. At the same time, instructors were not only paid too little but stretched too thin. In his second year on the faculty, in 1973, Steve Bartlett was given four courses to teach: world geography, black history, political theory and eighth-grade geometry. "No two of those was symbiotic," he says. McCallie was resting on its laurels to attract good teachers and strong applicants. "Charisma," says Curtis Baggett '65, who joined the faculty in 1972, "was the glue that held the school together when it was falling apart."

To turn the financial corner, McCallie needed more money than the school had ever raised. In March 1972, the board hired a professional fundraiser to direct the ambitious McCallie Development Fund campaign. By March 1974, the drive had received nearly $5 million in pledges, 75 percent of the goal, and the Board voted to begin construction of both a new academic building on a hillside site and a freestanding facility for the fine arts. The George Thomas Hunter Arts Building opened to students in late 1975, dedicated in memory of the man who established the local, philanthropic Benwood Foundation. The five-level Robert Maclellan Academic Center, which opened in the fall of 1976, was named for the man who served as vice chairman of the

McCallie Board of Trustees for 34 years until his death in 1971.

As the new academic building was preparing for occupancy in the late summer of 1976, energizing the McCallie community, Spencer III wrote, humorously, that "the old building will probably collapse the following day." He added: "Good teachers can teach almost anywhere, it is said, but we have stretched that point for too many years." North, Middle and South Hall did not fall by themselves; the rambling 80-yard-long repository of decades of boyhood memories took all summer to demolish. As workmen razed the building from south to north, the last section to fall was the northeast corner office that had been the sanctum of Major Burns for many years. "Let the record show," the retired Burns wrote on August 24, 1976, "that after a gallant, last-ditch fight, the N. Hall O.D. (officer of the day) office finally gave up."

"We're Brand New" trumpeted the 1977 *Pennant*, referring to the new academic center of campus, if not to the spirit of rejuvenation that accompanied it. The school finally had a modern teaching facility to fit its mission and reputation. Dedicated along with Maclellan Academic Center in October 1976 were Tate Hall, where a new north facade and entrance had been placed on the Junior School building that had long been the domain of Principal Russell Tate; and Spears Stadium, the 4,000-seat Alumni Field stands named for McCallie trustee and football All-American Bill Spears. Removal of the old academic building paved the way for a plant-filled quadrangle flanked by Maclellan Academic Center, Hunter Arts Center, Caldwell Hall and Tate Hall. Suddenly, McCallie looked more like a small college than a high school.

But McCallie needed more than new buildings; it needed to offer higher salaries to attract and retain excellent teachers. To help the school achieve its several goals, the Board followed Spencer III's recommendation and hired Mel Cooper in August 1975 as the school's first fulltime director of development. Cooper, who had been working for two older headmasters in Memphis, was attracted by the challenge and the enthusiastic brand of leadership at McCallie. His job would be to build both the the school's Sustaining Fund, which addressed student scholarships and faculty salaries, and its Development Fund, which covered large capital expenditures and contributed to the endowment.

"Mel and Spencer meshed perfectly," recalls Llewelyn Boyd '46, who became board chairman in 1976. "Mel was so valuable. Nationally, he was one of the most revered fund raisers in private secondary education. And he did it in such a low-key way."

Traveling as a team, Spencer and Cooper began visiting alumni throughout the South, describing dynamic changes on campus and McCallie's exciting vision for joining the nation's top tier of prep schools. In August 1977, the board launched the $6.8 million Capital Campaign Drive based on Spencer III's projected five-year cost for funding higher salaries, a lower student-teacher ratio, student scholarships and maintenance of the school's growing campus.

The majority of the funds raised were earmarked for the endowment, which would annually support these recurring needs. By May 1978, the campaign had received $3.5 million in pledges.

By McCallie's 75th anniversary in 1980, the school's outlook was bright. During the previous decade, the campus had been expanded by the acquisition of Central High School property along Dodds

McCallie moved from the Mid-South Association to the Tennessee State Secondary Athletic Association in 1971 and began competing successfully for state championships. The baseball team won the state crown in 1976, and the soccer team was state champion in 1978. In 1997, McCallie entered TSSAA's Division II for private schools.

Avenue. New playing fields were being created, and the school had maintained
its athletic prowess, competing now for state championships as a member of
the Tennessee Secondary School Athletic Association rather than as a member
of the defunct Mid-South Association, which McCallie left in 1971.

In 1980, the Board approved a 13 percent pay increase for the faculty and
would continued to raise salaries, even when it meant borrowing capital from
the endowment. As a result, McCallie was finding it easier to attract highly
qualified and motivated instructors, particularly in the sciences. Eventually, the
pay scale at McCallie would approach the top tenth of all schools in the
National Association of Independent Schools.

**One of the most beloved campus figures
for more than half a century was seventh-grade Bible teacher and varsity tennis coach John Strang, shown here with
students in 1979. Known to different
generations as "Bud" and "Yo," he was a
constant source of gentle words and
candy treats. Junior School introduced
seventh- and eighth-graders to some of
the school's most memorable teachers.**

McCallie had begun leasing, then buying computer equipment. It had
established an array of advanced placement courses, broadened its fine-arts
offerings and maintained a tradition of award-winning student publications.
Most importantly, it continued to define academic excellence in the South. The
1980 graduating class had 14 National Merit Scholarship Semifinalists, twice
the number of any other Chattanooga school and fully 10 percent of the senior
class itself. It was an accomplishment that would be repeated regularly.

How far the school would go from here was hard to imagine. Spencer III
recalls trying to visualize its future. "I sat in the stands in the evening one day
with the sun going down after being headmaster a couple of years and envisioned what the school would be at the turn of the century — and missed it
entirely," he says. "There was no way to know how much money would be
raised. It didn't occur to me how much would be done."

Chapter Six

Raising the Bar

1981-2004

A S THE 1980's ARRIVED, McCallie seemed a far cry from the bucolic campus that first beckoned boys in 1905. In more than 75 years of growth, the one-time family farm on Missionary Ridge had given way to an academic quadrangle and clusters of dormitories, gymnasiums and athletic fields. The streetcar that once wound its way through campus had vanished 30 years before, with McCallie science teacher Wallace Purdy the lone, nostalgic rider on the trolley's final midnight run. The lake was still a blue jewel but growing smaller, filled in to make space for a playing field. The city itself, which stopped two miles from McCallie in 1905, had decades ago jumped the Ridge and was now rushing miles to the east, pushing suburbs into the farmlands of East Brainerd, Collegedale and Ooltewah and into North Georgia.

Chapter Six

Opposite page: To provide space for additional athletic fields, land acquisition to the south (top of picture) became a school priority. Teachers such as Tom Boyd, at right, chairman of the science department, elevated academics and increased the array of advanced placement courses. At bottom, middle-school students relax between classes.

For McCallie, Chattanooga's growth was a mixed blessing. With land needed for a growing enrollment that now stood at 650, the school found itself surrounded by busy McCallie and Dodds avenues on the north and west, the Ridgedale neighborhood to the south and the steep upper slope of the Ridge above it. McCallie was confined to a 50-acre parcel not much larger than what existed at its founding and modest when compared to the sprawling campuses of some boarding schools. With literally no room for error, site plans for the placement of buildings at McCallie had always been meticulously developed and reviewed. But more space for fields and facilities was now needed to meet the demands of a broader sports and fitness program and of a student body that would number almost 900 by the new millennium.

Help came in an unlikely form. The market value of homes in Ridgedale had been declining for a decade, creating a neighborhood that was attracting some unsavory elements. In a defensive move, McCallie purchased two homes across narrow Union Avenue from the campus in 1980 to bring them under the school's control. "As soon as we bought the first two houses, the phone started ringing," recalls Mel Cooper, then the school's director of development. "Everyone wanted to sell us their property."

The school was happy to oblige. As homes appeared on the market, McCallie bought them, particularly prizing flat land at the bottom of the Ridge. With his courtly Southern drawl, Herbert Dunlap, who had retired from McCallie in 1972 after 47 years as commandant and business manager and was respected in the community as a former city commissioner of fire and police, helped McCallie negotiate with interested homeowners. Bit by bit, the school acquired parcels, including church and business properties on Dodds Avenue to add to the Central High property purchased 10 years before. Over the next two decades, the campus would double in size. Alumni who had not visited McCallie in years would be surprised and impressed at the transformation.

Growth, in fact, was the operative word for the school, not just in acreage but in the size of the Endowment and the annual goal of the Sustaining Fund; in faculty salaries, staffing numbers and enrichment programs; in advanced placement (AP) courses and academic chairs of excellence; in National Merit Semifinalists and publication awards; in enrollment and facilities. To say McCallie was on the move as the 1980's arrived is an understatement. The school was on a determined march to claim what it felt to be its rightful place among the best prep schools in America.

The $13.2 million Agenda for Excellence campaign launched by Trustees in 1983 and successfully completed in 1988 enlarged the Endowment, making possible permanent chairs of excellence to attract America's best high school educators. Along with the annual Sustaining Fund, which organized its first large-scale fall Phonathon in 1981, the Endowment supplemented faculty salaries so they continued to outpace inflation. The Campaign allowed for the renovation of the Chapel and Davenport Gym and the ongoing purchase of property for campus expansion.

Several years before and after Spencer McCallie III assumed the head-mastership in 1974, the school attracted a new, talented core of teachers and staff who would dedicate their entire careers to McCallie. (See Honor Roll, p. 113.) Under their direction, academic achievement and school morale climbed. Thus was McCallie in a strong position to deal with an issue confronting independent boys' schools across the

Coach Pete Potter celebrates the District 6 AAA championship with his 1985 football squad. For creating a resurgent McCallie football program, Potter was selected the Chattanooga area's Coach of the Decade for the 1980's. McCallie won the TSSAA Division II state championship in 2001 under Potter's son, Ralph.

country in the early 1980's. Because of a national "birth dearth," private schools found themselves fishing from a shrinking pool of applicants. McCallie and Baylor felt the effect as they battled for boys in the same market. To deal with the challenge, many traditionally all-boys schools began quietly considering coed enrollment, and Baylor publicly announced in May 1985 its decision to admit girls the fall of that year. The move, Baylor Associate Headmaster Doug Hale explained at the time, would "release Baylor from the dance of death with McCallie, competing for the very same kids every year."

Rehearsing are members of McCallie's Men's Ensemble, one of a dozen school musical groups that range from Handbells to the Honors Orchestra. The school's Coordinate Select Ensemble with GPS has performed at Carnegie Hall. Visual and performing arts at McCallie have continued to grow, and a new drama center opened in fall 2004.

McCallie and Chattanooga's other private, single-sex school, Girls Preparatory School, responded by linking arms and forming the McCallie/GPS Coordinate Program of academic, cultural, social and community activities. Upper class students from each school would have the opportunity to travel four miles to the other school for afternoon classes. (The formal student exchange would be replaced in 2000 by special coed courses, seminars, summer programs and academic retreats.) McCallie and GPS students would also jointly participate in theatrical and musical programs and enjoy a rich calendar of social events.

The Coordinate program gave McCallie students the best of both worlds: healthy interaction with girls from a "sister school" (an apt designation, as the McCallie founders' sister, Grace, was a co-founder of GPS) and the "powerful culture" of all-boys schooling, where, as Spencer put it, "there are fewer distractions, more openness and a greater sense of purpose. Boys are active learners," he elaborated, "their humor is different, and they'll talk about feelings more openly in an all-boys' class than if girls were there." The compromise worked; McCallie's enrollment figures continued to grow.

During the 1980's, the school's development office, under Mel Cooper's direction, proved capable of raising substantial funds from a large and loyal

base of alumni, including those living far beyond Chattanooga. "Mel significantly raised our sights in strategic planning," says Curtis Baggett. The Board of Trustees, meanwhile, grew emboldened in approving goals. A five-year strategic plan unveiled in 1987 called for faculty salaries to climb beyond the top 25th percentile among NAIS schools and the Endowment to grow significantly so financial aid could be bolstered (boarding tuition had topped $10,000 by 1986), more minority students could be recruited and additional chairs of excellence could be created.

Physical changes were also addressed. The campus was to be enlarged by adding fields for soccer, baseball, intramural sports and lacrosse, and a new main entrance was to be constructed on Dodds Avenue. The centerpiece of the campus transformation was a $13.2 million sports and activity center. Summing up the ambitious plan, Trustee and future Board Chairman Hardwick Caldwell, Jr., '40 declared, "McCallie is not a stand-still school."

The goals coalesced in the $35 million PACE (for People-Athletics-

While the school's Sustaining Fund increased student scholarships and faculty salaries, the $36 million PACE Campaign reshaped the campus. In 1991, students outlined the soon-to-be-constructed Sports and Activity Center. Headmaster Spencer McCallie III and Director of Development Mel Cooper check blueprints during construction of the building that emerged (opposite page).

Campus-Endowment) Campaign announced in 1988 as the largest fund-raising endeavor by an independent school in Tennessee. The Campaign eventually received $36.2 million, and the award-winning athletic complex was dedicated on February 12, 1993, giving McCallie a new signature edifice and source of pride.

Atlanta-based media pioneer Ted Turner '56 declared in a biography written of him that McCallie, which he attended as a six-year boarding student, helped shape his life, and he described McCallie as "one of the best and toughest schools in the South." Nearly 40 years later, his statement seemed truer still. A survey of McCallie parents conducted by an outside consulting firm in 1994 showed strong support for the school, with special praise for its academic challenge and quality of the faculty. In her summary, the project consultant declared: "I have conducted over 75 surveys to date and have never seen such a positive response."

Data supported the parents' impression. The U.S. Department of Education named McCallie a National School of Excellence in 1989, one of 42 non-public schools to receive the national designation that year. The number of AP scholars and National Merit Semifinalists reported by the school each year consistently ranked at or near the top of all schools in the state. An impressive number of McCallie students represented Tennessee as Presidential Scholars and were among the 20 students selected annually from across the country to attend the American Chemical Society Chemistry Olympiad. "What it means," said then-Dean of Studies Miles McNiff of the honors, including annually high average student-body scores on SAT and AP exams, "is that our students, whether taking AP courses or the normal curriculum, are learning more and more and are being better and better prepared for college."

McCallie maintained its focus on developing boys not only in mind but in body, character and spirit. The

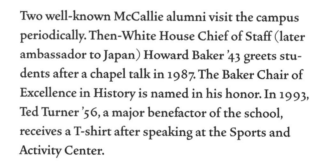

Two well-known McCallie alumni visit the campus periodically. Then-White House Chief of Staff (later ambassador to Japan) Howard Baker '43 greets students after a chapel talk in 1987. The Baker Chair of Excellence in History is named in his honor. In 1993, Ted Turner '56, a major benefactor of the school, receives a T-shirt after speaking at the Sports and Activity Center.

Honor Code, adopted in 1906, had, with some modifications, stood the test of time. Harsher provisions that required boys to report fellow students for Code violations and demanded an apology to the entire student body from those found guilty were dropped in the 1970's, but the Code's insistence that students act with honor and integrity or withdraw from the McCallie community remained. Students were still taken at their word when they signed the Pledge, edited several times over a century, that stated: "This work is my own. I have neither given nor received any unauthorized help." Recommended punishment for a student found guilty of a second honor offense was expulsion.

The school continued to emphasize the spiritual side of life. Devotionals were presented several mornings a week, Bible class credits were still required for graduation, boarding students had to attend a weekend religious service appropriate to their faith, and the school motto remained unchanged: "Man's chief end is to glorify God and enjoy Him forever." At the same time, students were encouraged to genuinely explore their religious beliefs — to come to own them and not accept them by rote. And most commendably, McCallie's transmission of Judeo-Christian values and ethics through the study of the Bible was presented in such a way that it could be accepted as an enriching experience for families of a wide range of faiths, as the school's multi-religious student body attested to year after year.

McCallie enhanced its physical activities to encompass the needs of all students. From its founding, the school had promoted interscholastic competition for building strength and character. But the school came to realize that 40 percent of boys never participated in any of 13 varsity sports offered at McCallie. To meet their need for physical activity and competition, the school launched an intramural program in 1977 that was broadened in 1994 when McCallie Tornado Athletics was established. MTA combined personal fitness, intramural team sports and development of skills for

McCallie's nationally-ranked crew team skims the Tennessee River.

lifetime sports. With the Sports and Activity Center and two new intramural baseball diamonds at its disposal, MTA was able to fulfill the founders' goal for their students: a sound mind in a sound body.

As Spencer McCallie III neared the end of a 25-year tenure as headmaster that was already filled with major accomplishments, two momentous programs were announced. In May 1995, he described to the Board of Trustees the critical need for a new building to house the seventh- and eighth-grade junior school. It had outgrown Tate Hall, one of the oldest buildings on campus, whose classrooms were small and labs "woefully lacking." At the same time, he noted that the Hamilton County School System was reorganizing its middle schools to include grade six as well as seven and eight. This meant that a county school student who wanted to attend McCallie would have to make two school changes in two years to do so: from grammar school to middle school in the sixth grade and from middle school to McCallie in the seventh.

Shouldn't McCallie establish a full middle school by adding a sixth grade and offer the faculty, facilities and curriculum to make it one of the finest programs in the South? That idea bore fruit in April 1997 when the school announced plans for a $7 million building to house 270 middle-school students. Construction of McDonald Hall began in 1998 on the site of the old tennis courts on Kyle Street overlooking the lake. In fall 1999, the building was dedicated in memory of John McDonald and in honor of his wife, Dorcas, parents of John H. '50 and Jack '51. The McDonald Hall naming recognized the couple's pivotal role in the school's early efforts at campus planning. McCallie's first class of sixth graders in eight decades took their seats in the new building. Not since the Little Shavers, as members of McCallie's early fifth- and sixth-grade primary department were known, had students so young been on campus. With their addition, McCallie's total enrollment jumped from 780 to 880 in one year.

As the Middle School program took shape, the school embarked on an innovative project that would affect the quality of the Boarding Department and Upper School. The brainchild of Ed Michaels III '60 and Alan Dickson '49, the Honors Scholarship Program was modeled after the University of North Carolina's Morehead Scholarship and similar merit-based grants offered to highly qualified entering freshmen by Vanderbilt, Emory, Virginia and Duke. McCallie would bring the idea to the high school level to attract some of the country's most talented ninth and tenth graders — boys who excelled in leadership as well as academics. In doing so, the school would raise the caliber of the student body and spread the McCallie name nationwide.

Under Ed Michael's vigorous leadership, the school set a $10 million goal for funding 20 full scholarships based on merit. The first two full-scholarship recipients, one from Denver, CO and the other from Winston-Salem, NC, entered McCallie in fall 1998, but they didn't come alone. Seventeen of the 25 finalists for the scholarships that year also decided to attend McCallie, though 80 percent had never heard of the school before visiting the campus. This "draft effect," as it was called, occurred year after year, and the annual infusion of Honors Scholarship talent was quickly felt. In 2002, the Board reported that the program had a "profoundly positive effect on the life of McCallie," from reducing disciplinary cases to improving academic performance. "The program has turned around the boarding department," declares former Board

Chairman Dr. David McCallie. "SAT's go up every year."

While the school was adding new programs and departments, it could point with pride to the growing stability of the faculty. As salaries and development programs had improved, tenures had lengthened. Compared to McCallie's earliest days, when the school was considered a launch pad for ambitious teachers, it was now viewed as a coveted destination, one of the best secondary schools in America to call a permanent home. By 2004, a total of 34 members of the faculty had been with the school 20 years or more, creating the strongest nucleus in its history.

In 1996, Spencer McCallie III had served official notice that he would retire as headmaster in the summer of 1999. One of the most highly regarded secondary-school educators in the country, he had been elected president of both the Southern Association of Independent Schools and the national Headmasters' Association. At McCallie, he had overseen the growth of the Endowment from $350,000 to $40 million and the expansion of the campus from less than 50 to more than 100 acres. Most importantly, he had raised salaries to attract and retain a highly professional faculty. He had guided the school with a trademark sense of humor, a relaxed style and a strong presence. His clear vision had drawn strong support from trustees and alumni and elevated McCallie to the front ranks of preparatory schools nationwide.

The issue facing the Board's seven-person search committee as it began considering a successor was who would be willing to follow a headmaster of legendary accomplishment and, in addition, be the first non-McCallie family member to take the reins of the school. A consultant thought the assignment so daunting that McCallie should consider naming an interim headmaster to bridge the gap. But the search committee disagreed. "We felt it would be a real disservice to the school, that we would lose so much momentum," said Committee Co-Chairman Hal Daughdrill III '73.

◆◆◆

In the fall of 1998, Dr. Kirk Walker, Jr.'69, headmaster of the private Ensworth School, a kindergarten-through-eighth-grade academy in Nashville, TN, received a call from Hal Daughdrill asking if Walker would allow his name to be entered in the McCallie headmaster search. "I felt if doing so would help the process, that was fine with me," says Dr. Walker, "but I was certain they could find a remarkable candidate among the others who had applied." The Committee's nationwide search had indeed yielded 50 applicants that were culled to 20 for serious consideration. But as Committee members sifted through resumes and conducted interviews, they began to realize that the ideal candidate might be in their midst.

Kirk Walker, who had been a trustee of the McCallie Board since 1994, enjoyed long, impressive ties to the school. As a six-year McCallie day student, he had been valedictorian of his class, captain of the debate team, president of Cum Laude, secretary of Keo-Kio, a member of the Student Council, a captain in the military and editor of the *Tornado*. He attended the University of North Carolina as a Morehead Scholar, graduating Phi Beta Kappa in 1972, and earned a Ph.D. in education from Peabody College of Vanderbilt University.

His career brought him back to Chattanooga in 1982 when he became headmaster of The Bright School, one of McCallie's feeder elementary schools. He moved to Nashville in 1990 to accept the position at Ensworth, where he built strong academic and athletic programs, established a significant endowment and oversaw major improvements in facilities. His reputation climbed with his accomplishments, earning him the presidency of the Tennessee Association of Independent Schools. Yet, while build-

---

Dr. Kirk Walker, Jr. '69 returned to his Alma Mater in 1999 to become the first person outside the McCallie family to serve as headmaster. Under his guidance, the school has maintained its ascendant course.

---

ing a strong professional resume in Chattanooga and Nashville, he continued to serve as a dedicated McCallie alumnus, calling for the annual Phonathon, serving on the Sustaining Fund Cabinet, heading the Nashville Honors Scholarship Selection Committee and joining the Board of Trustees. No higher endorsement of the school could be given than when he and his wife, Patsi, sent their eldest son, Rob '99, to McCallie as a boarding student.

Selected a finalist for the McCallie headmaster's post, Kirk Walker visited the campus one weekend and confirmed his keenly felt sense of affiliation with the school and its mission. He and his wife saw faculty members who had been a positive influence on Rob, then in his senior year, just as McCallie teachers had been role models for Dr. Walker in his student days. "The McCallie community is very special," he says. "I'm continually overwhelmed by the faculty's and staff's devotion to McCallie and its boys."

Though the 47-year-old Walker had never been headmaster of a high school or a boarding school, the Search Committee felt strongly it had found the right person. The Board's unanimous confirmation of Walker was greeted with an impromptu, celebratory chorus of the McCallie hymnal favorite, "Love Lifted Me," by members of the Committee. Ward Nelson '75, who was involved in the search process, described Dr. Walker's interview answers as having been thoughtful, direct and honest "yet with some humor and humility. I immediately thought, 'He's just going to be a godsend to the school.'" For Kirk Walker, the McCallie position beckoned with a sense of deep purpose. Before the Board's final decision, he had listed reasons to stay in Nashville, where he had popular support, or to move to McCallie. Under reasons for going, he wrote, simply: "I think I'm supposed to." It came down to a matter of the heart.

In the fall of 1999, thirty years after graduating, Dr. Walker returned to his alma mater as headmaster in a year of change. He was far from the only newcomer on campus. A robust contingent of 13 teachers had joined the faculty, and the sixth grade was beginning its first year in newly dedicated, state-of-the-art McDonald Hall, which gave the 264 Middle School students a feeling of equality with the Upper School. Before Kirk Walker presided over his first roll-call of graduating seniors at McCallie's spring 2000 commencement, the Board was praising the "seamless transition" of administrations. Said Mel Cooper: "We didn't skip a beat."

In fact, the spectrum of student accomplishment only seemed to increase. "We've got to keep raising the bar on our expectations about the kind of school we want to be and the kind of national reputation we want to have," the new headmaster declared, and students responded. The school claimed 12 of the 24 National Merit Semifinalists in the city and county in the fall of 2001. That fall, winter and spring, McCallie won eight state championships: football, cross-country, climbing, debate, crew, swimming, wrestling and lacrosse. During Kirk Walker's first two years, the school could boast of producing the "Best Multi-Issue High School Literary Magazine" in the country, as the *Argonaut* was judged by the American Scholastic Press Association, and fielding the fourth-best prep-school swimming and diving team in the nation, as ranked by *Swim World* magazine. The crew team rowed on the River Thames in the invitation-only Henley Royal Regatta, and the McCallie/GPS choral ensemble sang in repeat performances at Carnegie Hall.

McCallie emphasized to boys the importance of fostering a strong school community, with its code of honor and spirit of respect, while cultivating a sense of obligation to the larger community. McCallie's Cultural Celebration broke new ground in 2003 when both the Upper and Middle schools devoted an entire day to intense examination of diversity and commonalities among people of different races and religions. Students, meanwhile, continued looking beyond their campus by participating in a variety of community service projects, from tutoring children of low-income households and serving as Big Brothers on weekends, to clearing neighborhoods of debris and building Habitat for Humanity houses.

In the midst of the school's full-speed agenda, the death of Spencer McCallie, Jr. in July 2001 at the age of 92 vividly recalled a bygone era. "Dr. Spence" had served as headmaster for 25 years, from 1949 until his retirement in 1974, and had continued as a member of the Board of Trustees until 1990. For several thousand graduates, he had been the face and soul of the school. One alumnus wrote that Spencer McCallie instilled in a boy "the ability to look the world and men in the eye," and a professional colleague referred to him as "a headmaster's headmaster." Spencer III said of his father: "Many of us here were blessed by his strong conviction, by straightforward, simple talk – by the extraordinarily clear example of his life — but we had fun, too. The world will miss a man like that."

Legendary teachers who left their mark on decades of students were also passing from the scene. The school mourned the deaths of Eliott Schmidt, the ebullient, pipe-smoking history teacher and debate coach who spent 40 years at McCallie; of Thomas Walker '25, who spent 31 years teaching language and directing school plays, and his wife, Mary Louise, a Latin instructor and assis-

Building a Habitat for Humanity house with GPS students is a community service activity sponsored by the McCallie/GPS Coordinate Program. It allows students from both schools to jointly participate in academic, athletic, cultural and social programs and events. Outreach at McCallie includes serving as Big Brothers and tutoring students from low-income neighborhoods.

tant librarian for 35 years; of John Day, who taught seventh-grade geography and history, coached football and track, and served as Junior School principal in a 34-year McCallie career; and of John Strang, who for 54 years made the seventh-grade Bible class one of the most enjoyable courses a student would ever take. Atop his coffin as it was wheeled from the sanctuary of the church was an emblem of the gentle words and hard, wrapped treats he had endearingly dispensed to a half-century of young men — a dish of candy.

The transformation of the campus was a work in progress. In 2002, the school began construction of a $7 million, 32,000-square-foot dining hall three times as spacious as aging Alumni Hall. Designed as the "living room" of the community, the building was lofty in style, with vaulted ceilings of exposed wood

Dedicated in the spring of 2004, the new dining hall replaced 62-year-old Alumni Hall and gave students, faculty and staff a place to nourish body and spirit. Perched on a hill overlooking the city and regarded as the "living room" of the campus community, it offers an airy setting for conversation and fellowship.

beams and windows overlooking a patio with a panoramic view of the city and mountains beyond. "The campus will be bookended on the north by the Chapel and on the south by this dining hall," Dr. Walker said at the groundbreaking. "One place feeds the spirit. The other feeds the body. Both build community." Upon completion in the spring of 2004, the building drew praise. "You've given McCallie a place where boys will linger," said Board Chairman Hal Daughdrill III to alumni attending the dedication luncheon. "Whenever students and teachers get together, that's where the magic of McCallie occurs."

McCallie magic was evident in the support for successive capital campaigns that had produced dramatic growth in the Endowment, faculty salaries, financial aid and campus facilities. In 1999, the Council for the Advancement and Support of Education (CASE) awarded McCallie its prestigious Circle of Excellence in Educational Fund-Raising Award. In 2001, McCallie Vice President of Planning and Board Relations Mel Cooper received the Robert Bell Crow Memorial Award presented annually by CASE for distinguished achievement in independent school development. A school that had scratched to raise money in its early years had become a national model for working with patrons to accomplish inspiring objectives.

As the school enters its second century, it has identified important reasons to continue growing the Endowment: for need-based financial aid so McCallie can remain accessible to talented, deserving boys; for modern academic facilities so students have the best classroom environment, whether for studying the sciences or the arts; for new dormitories so McCallie can continue to attract outstanding students from across the nation; and for faculty recruitment and development that ensures the finest teachers and teaching methods for the next generation of McCallie student.

During a century of educating boys, McCallie has changed dramatically in physical appearance and breadth of curriculum, but its values are those of the founders. Through 10 decades of technological advances and social transformation, honor, truth and duty remain the bywords of the school. That such simple and noble words endure is remarkable, but, if anything, they've grown in importance. "Today, McCallie's mission of developing character has never been more relevant because the transition from boyhood to manhood has never been more daunting," Kirk Walker explains. "Boys today are bombarded by the values of popular culture, a culture which celebrates fame, not achievement; celebrities, not contributing citizens; the counterfeit, not the authentic." Through the study of Judeo-Christian values, McCallie seeks to instill in young men the virtues of relating with justice and compassion to the world around them.

In this mission, the school has been guided by a Board of Trustees with a rare ability to work together to advance the needs of the school and its students. As Chairman Hal Daughdrill is fond of telling new trustees: "At McCallie Board meetings, it's as if everyone's ego has been checked at the door." Kirk Walker regards the Board as historically one of the school's greatest strengths. "It is a Board," he says, "that always wanted to find the best solution for McCallie, that

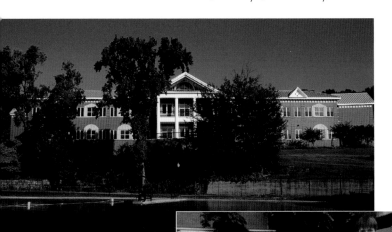

Situated above McCallie Lake, McDonald Hall is one of the first views visitors get as they wind their way into campus. From faculty recruitment and character development to enhanced academic, athletic and residential facilities, McCallie has been successful in creating an experience that inspires and nurtures the best in young men.

would honor the past and make the most sense for the future."

As McCallie is reflected in the lives of boys who became men under its tutelage – in their values, their work ethic, their striving to build a better world – so, too, do the men who have left McCallie reflect upon the school. "Every alumnus carries a two- or four- or six-year snapshot of the school's history with them," observes Herb Cohn '49 of the vivid and formative experience that is McCallie, "and it has affected our lives ever since." Arranged in an album, these individual snapshots – of boys in the dress of different eras, standing with different teachers against different backdrops – share a common feature. Call it a sense of integrity and moral purpose. For a century now, that is the face of McCallie.

Chronology

1905   Spencer and Park McCallie open McCallie School in a makeshift schoolhouse on Missionary Ridge in Chattanooga with four teachers and 58 boys in grades 9-12. (September 21)

       McCallie School is incorporated as a family-owned, for-profit organization. (December 6)

1906   McCallie Honor System is established. (January)

       Three-story School Building, later known as Middle Hall, is completed for fall term.

1907   Douglas Hall dormitory is added to the campus.

1908   Largest crowd to attend a local football game watches McCallie and Baylor play to a scoreless tie at Chamberlain Field.

1909   First McCallie Alumni Association meeting is held at Patten Hotel.

1916   Alumni Field, including fifth-mile track, tennis courts and outdoor gym, is dedicated.

1918   McCallie introduces military training in response to America's ill-preparedness in World War I.

       Lt. Clifford Barker Grayson is killed in combat. The Grayson Memorial Medal is established to annually honor the school's most highly regarded senior student.

1919   North and South Halls are added to each end of the School Building. McCallie fall enrollment is 280 students from 13 states.

1921   T.E.P. Woods joins the faculty as associate headmaster, a post he holds for 26 years.

       First football team to be called the "Blue Tornado" has a 7-0 season.

1924   The cement-block gym is completed near the lake.

1925   Chalmers McIlwaine, Arthur Lee Burns, Herbert Dunlap and William Wallace Purdy join the faculty.

1930   The Privilege Rating System is implemented by T.E.P. Woods.

       The Alma Mater, written by Arthur Burns and arranged by Wallace Purdy, is published.

1933   McCallie holds first annual Mother's Day Parade.

1935   Spencer McCallie Jr. and Robert McCallie are members of the faculty after earning master's degrees at Duke University.

1937   McCallie files a revised state charter as a non-profit educational corporation privately held by the new Board of Trustees. (September 8)

1939   The Missionary Committee is established; initial funds help Kashing High School in China. Keo-Kio is created to recognize senior leadership.

1940   McCallie and Baylor play their last football game until 1971.

1942   Alumni Hall is completed.

1945   Sixty-two alumni die in military service during World War II.

       Professor Spencer McCallie retires, leaving Doctor Park McCallie as sole headmaster.

1947   First Sustaining Fund drive is held.

1949   Professor Spencer McCallie dies of leukemia (October 18) at age 74, a few days after teaching his Old Testament Bible Class to seventh-grade students.

       Doctor Park McCallie retires as headmaster. William Pressly, Spencer McCallie, Jr. and Robert McCallie serve as a Board of Headmasters until July 1951, when Pressly leaves McCallie, making Robert and Spencer, Jr. co-headmasters.

       Davenport Gymnasium is dedicated.

1951   Hutcheson Hall is dedicated.

1953   Maclellan Hall is dedicated.

1955   McCallie Chapel is dedicated.

1958   Junior School Building is dedicated.

       Sophomore leadership society, TEPS, is formed.

1959   Goree Nelson Memorial Indoor Pool is dedicated.

1962   Publisher Hodding Carter inaugurates the Vann Lecture Series.

1963   Belk Hall is dedicated. Founder's Home is expanded.

1964   Caldwell Hall is dedicated.

1965   Robert McCallie dies of a heart attack (November 22) at age 54 after serving as co-headmaster for 17 years. Spencer McCallie, Jr. becomes the school's sole headmaster.

1970   Board of Trustees approves an open-admissions policy. David Chatman '75 of Louisville, KY is the school's first African-American graduate.

Board of Trustees votes to drop military training "to enable the school to broaden curriculum offerings."

Chalmers McIlwaine '21 is the first recipient of the school's Distinguished Alumnus Award.

1971 Dr. James Park McCallie, co-founder and president emeritus of the school, dies at age 91. (June 6)

McCallie purchases abandoned Central High School property on Dodds Avenue.

Distinguished Alumnus Award goes to Howard Baker '43 and William Brock III '49, the only two U.S. Senators serving at the same time from the same state who attended the same prep school.

McCallie leaves the Mid-South Athletic Association for the Tennessee Secondary School Athletic Association.

1972 Arthur Lee Burns and Herbert Dunlap retire.

1974 Spencer McCallie, Jr. retires as headmaster at age 65, succeeded by Spencer McCallie III. Also retiring is Chalmers McIlwaine.

1976 Hunter Arts Building is dedicated. (April)

Maclellan Academic Center, Tate Hall and Spears Stadium are dedicated, and the quadrangle is created. (October)

1977 McCallie begins an intramural program.

1980 Alumni Hall is remodeled.

1981 McCallie Phonathon is organized on a large scale for the first time.

1985 McCallie and Girls Preparatory School announce Coordinate Program of academic exchange and social activities.

1987 John L. Strang Tennis Center is dedicated in honor of the longtime faculty member and varsity tennis coach.

1988 Agenda for Excellence campaign surpasses $13.2 million goal.

1989 McCallie is selected a National School of Excellence by the U.S. Department of Education.

McCallie announces five-year PACE (People-Athletics-Campus-Endowment) Campaign. The $35 million goal is the highest ever set by an independent school in Tennessee.

1990 McCallie senior class has 19 National Merit Semifinalists, including two with perfect SAT scores.

Football coach Pete Potter is named Chattanooga area's "Coach of the Decade."

Houston Patterson '43 and Warren James '43 retire as associate headmasters.

1991 *When We Came To The Ridge*, written by George Hazard, Jr. '64, is published.

1992 Irwin Belk Track is dedicated.

1993 The $13 million Sports and Activities Center, center-

piece of the PACE campaign, is dedicated.

1994 New main entrance to school on Dodds Avenue is completed.

MTA (McCallie Tornado Athletics) is created for students not involved in one of the school's 13 varsity sports.

1997 Spencer McCallie III is elected president of the national Headmasters' Association. He is former president of the Southern Association of Independent Schools.

McCallie begins membership in new prep-school Division II of the Tennessee Secondary School Athletic Association.

1998 The Honors Scholarship Program, offering merit-based scholarships to boarding students from across the country, begins with the first ninth- and tenth-grade recipients.

A search committee is created by the Board of Trustees to find a successor to Spencer McCallie III, who will retire as headmaster at the end of the 1998-99 school year.

1999 Dr. Robert Kirk Walker, Jr. '69 becomes the first non-McCallie family member to serve as McCallie headmaster.

McCallie enrolls its first class of sixth graders as it opens $7 million McDonald Hall, the new home of the Middle School.

McCallie receives the 1999 Circle of Excellence in Educational Fund-Raising Award from the national Council for the Advancement and Support of Education (CASE).

2000 McCallie/GPS Coordinate Program replaces regular campus exchange of students with special coed courses, roundtables, summer programs and academic retreats.

2001 Dr. Spencer McCallie, Jr., headmaster from 1949 to 1974, dies at age 92. (July 13)

The *Argonaut* is named "Best Multi-Issue High School Literary Magazine" by the American Scholastic Press Association.

McCallie's football team joins seven other school teams (cross-country, climbing, debate, swimming, crew, wrestling and lacrosse) in claiming state championships in 2001-02.

2003 McCallie's enrollment has grown to 880, including 231 boarding students from 17 states and four foreign countries. Forty-six boarders are Honors Scholars.

2004 The school's new $7 million, 32,000-square-foot dining hall is dedicated. It will serve as the "living room" of the campus community.

Thirty-three students are named National Merit Semifinalists or receive National Merit Commendation.

Ridgedale Gym is converted to a theater, providing a new home for the Drama Department.

McCallie begins a series of events celebrating the school's 2005 Centennial Year.

Honor Roll

McCallie School Board of Trustees
Founding member

Honor Roll

Charles Ralph Ewing 1956 – 1980

Thomas A. Fanjoy '50 1985 – 1993, 2004 –

Edward M. Fisher '51 1971 – 1974, 1975 – 1984

* Dr. George Allen Fleece '27 1937 – 1938

* John Storrs Fletcher 1937 – 1961

A. C. Frame, Jr. 1972 – 1975

Thomas W. Francescon, Sr. 1995 – 1997

Mrs. Thomas W. Francescon, Sr. 1995 – 1997

Roger William Frank '36 1955 – 1957

Selmon T. Franklin, Jr. 1977 – 1979

James F. Gallivan, Jr. '76 1993 – 2003

Warren S. Gardner, Jr. '42 1971 – 1972, 1975 – 1987

Dr. Robert E. Giles, Jr. '64 1980 – 1987

Dr. E. Wayne Gilley 1968 – 1969

Mrs. E. Wayne Gilley 1968 – 1969

Dr. William C. Greer 1988 – 1989

Mrs. William C. Greer 1988 – 1989

George W. Gwaltney '77 1990 – 1996

W. C. Haisten, Jr. 1992 – 1995

Mrs. W. C. Haisten, Jr. 1992 – 1995

Drew E. Haskins, Jr. 1976

Dr. Drewry E. Haskins III '64 1985 – 1988

Dr. Joseph M. Haskins '76 1996 – 1997

Charles A. Hawkins '49 1981 – 1983

Mark Hanna Hays, Jr. '40 1963

Charles E. Hickey 1970 – 1972

Dr. F. Barry Hodges III '61 1990 – 1993

Dr. C. Wayne Holley, Jr. '77 2003 –

J. Kyle Holley, Jr. '44 1972 – 1981

Henry A. Hoss 1989 – 1992

Mrs. Henry A. Hoss 1989 – 1992

Albert D. Huddleston '70 1993 – 1996

Hugh D. Huffaker, Jr. '48 1972 – 1986

Hugh Dayton Huffaker 1956 – 1972

Robert F. Huffaker, Jr. '78 2004 –

Dr. Noel C. Hunt III '54 1960

* John LaFayette Hutcheson, Jr. '20 1937 – 1975

John LaFayette Hutcheson III '47 1967 – 1976

Theodore Montague Hutcheson '60 1978 – 1981

R. P. Jackson 1981 – 1983

Mrs. R. P. Jackson 1981 – 1983

Donald Lloyd Jones '33 1961

Robert Cannon Jones, Jr. '14 1957 – 1967

Robert C. Jones III '44 1972 – 1984

Robert C. Jones IV '74 1996 – 1997

Morton J. Kent 1969 – 1970

Robert Sterling Killebrew 1963 – 1977

James W. Lail '45 1979 – 1986, 1988 – 1990

E. Cody Laird, Jr. '53 1982 – 1985

Edward Hicks Lannom, Jr. '42 1982 – 1988

H. Grant Law, Jr. '64 1988 – 1990

Fred W. Lazenby '50 1988 – 1999

Leighton LeBoeuf 1985 – 1988

Mrs. Leighton LeBoeuf 1985 – 1988

Charles B. Lebovitz '55 1979 – 1987, 1994 – 2000

Michael I. Lebovitz '82 2000 –

Howard I. Levine '56 1993 – 2002, 2003 –

W. N. Lillios 1990 – 1993

Mrs. W. N. Lillios 1990 – 1993

Robert L. Lockaby, Jr. '71 1993 – 1996

Dr. Edward C. Loughlin, Jr. '52 1985 – 1991

Hugh Owen Maclellan '30 1961 – 1988, 1989 – 1994

H. O. Maclellan, Jr. '57 1977 – 1983

* Robert Llewellyn Maclellan '24 1937 – 1971

John M. Martin 1978 – 1981

Allen L. McCallie '73 1990 – 1991, 2000 –

Dr. David P. McCallie '40 1971 – 1983, 1985 – 1997, 1998 –

* Dr. James Park McCallie 1937 – 1971

* Ms. Margaret Ellen McCallie 1937 – 1948

* Dr. Robert Lewis McCallie '29 1937 – 1965

Spencer J. McCallie III '55 1972 – 1997

* Prof. Spencer Jarnagin McCallie 1937 – 1949

* Dr. Spencer Jarnagin McCallie, Jr. '28 1937 – 1990

Thomas Crane McCallie '10 1953 – 1959

John W. McCravey, M.D. '66 1990 – 1992

John H. McDonald '50 1995 – 2001

Joseph Hastings McGinness '35 1953 – 1954

William Scott McGinness '31 1948 – 1949

W. Scott McGinness, Jr. '65 1986 – 1989

Richard D. McRae, Jr. '66 2000 – 2003

James Ransom McWane '50 1969 – 1972

Ronald S. Mercer '60 1980 – 1982, 1988 – 1989

Edward G. Michaels III '60 1990 –

* James E. Millis 1937

James Henry Millis '41 1960 – 1971, 1989 – 1994

Olan Mills II '48 1972 – 1990, 1991 – 1997, 1998 –

Frank M. Mitchener, Jr. '51 1984 – 1986

William Lasley Montague '31 1959

Ansley H. Moses '48 1976 – 1979

Dr. Robert Goree Nelson '12 1947 – 1969

Dr. N. R. Nichols III 1971 – 1974

Irvin Overton, Sr. 1990 – 1996

Mrs. Irvin Overton, Sr. 1990 – 1996

John G. Palmer 1981 – 1984

Mrs. John G. Palmer 1981 – 1984

John C. Parham '58 1982 – 1985

Terrence S. Parks '61 1983 – 1989

Ward Petty '80 1992 – 1995

Mervin Pregulman 1974 – 1984

Dr. Paul M. Pressly 1994 – 1997

Dr. William Laurens Pressly 1943 – 1956

Daniel F. Provine, Jr. 1993 – 1996

Mrs. Daniel F. Provine, Jr. 1993 – 1996

Marcus H. Rafiee '80 1995 – 2001

Daniel B. Rather '53 1979 – 1982, 2003 –

W. Mark Reynolds 1994 – 1997

Mrs. W. Mark Reynolds 1994 – 1997

James C. Richards '77 1991 – 1994

Harry T. Robinson III '70 1995 – 1997

T. Jack Robinson '55 1983 – 1989, 1994 – 2000

J. Hoyle Rymer '62 1988 – 1994

Rodolph G. Sherrill '56 1984 – 1992

Seth Walker Sizer '46 1965 – 1966

Charles G. Smith '70 1991 – 1994

Blackwell Smith, Jr. '48 1971 – 1980

Gordon L. Smith, Jr. '43 1968 – 1970, 1974 – 1988,
   1989 – 1995, 1996 – 2002

Gordon L. Smith III '72 1988 – 1991, 1995 – 2001

James F. Smith, Jr. '47 1995 – 2001

William Douglas Spears '24 1960 – 1985

Richard W. Spencer '51 1974 – 1984

William A. Spencer, Jr. '38 1974 – 1984

W. Lloyd Stanley, Jr. 1986 – 1989

Mrs. W. Lloyd Stanley, Jr. 1986 – 1989

David A. Stonecipher '59 1996 –

Ewing Strang '71 1983 – 1986

Timothy A. Stump '75 1996 – 2004

Robert Campbell Taylor, Sr. '48 1975 – 1984

Richard C. Thatcher, Jr. '33 1961 – 1962, 1969 – 1979

* Dr. Richard Frederick Thomason 1937 – 1965

Herbert A. Thornbury '63 1987 – 1990, 1991 – 1994

Charles E. Tindell, Jr. 1996 – 1997

Mrs. Charles E. Tindell, Jr. 1996 – 1997

Prentis Tomlinson, Jr. '61 1983 – 1989

Harold L. Turner 1982 – 1985

Mrs. Marie N. Turner 1982 – 1985

Thomas W. Wade, Jr. '52 1983 – 1986

Dr. Robert Kirk Walker, Sr. 1968

R. Kirk Walker, Jr., Ph.D. '69 1994 – 1998, 1999 –

Robert J. Walker '58 1984 – 1990, 2004 –

William Edward Walker, Jr. '46 1969 – 1975, 1987 – 1993

James Creekmore Wann '40 1968

Edward Hornsby Wasson '22 1957 – 1969

Jack L. Webb, Jr. '75 1980 – 1985, 1990 – 1992

C. Randolph Wedding '52 1973 – 1979

Alexander White Wells '37 1963 – 1964

Jack Erwin Whitaker '23 1951 – 1973

Thomas A. Williams, Sr. 1987 – 1991

Mrs. Thomas A. Williams, Sr. 1987 – 1991

J. C. Wilson III '55 1983 – 1984

Mark King Wilson, Jr. '29 1947 – 1969

Colon W. York 1971 – 1979

Distinguished Alumnus Award Recipients

Chalmers Moore Stirling McIlwaine '21 1970

Ambassador Howard H. Baker, Jr. '43 1971

Sen. William E. Brock III '49 1971

Arthur Lee Burns '20 1972

Col. Herbert Pritchard Dunlap 1972

John LaFayette Hutcheson, Jr. '20 1973

Dr. Spencer Jarnagin McCallie, Jr. '28 1974

Hugh Owen Maclellan '30 1975

William Emerson Brock, Jr. '21 1976

Charles Ralph Ewing 1976

William Douglas Spears '24 1977

Dr. James H. Daughdrill, Jr. '52 1978

Hardwick Caldwell, Jr. '40 1979

Hon. Gillespie V. Montgomery '39 1980

William Edward Walker, Jr. '46 1981

Olan Mills II '48 1982

Robert E. Turner '56 1983

Llewellyn Boyd '46 1984

Dr. David P. McCallie '40 1985

William B. Dunavant, Jr. '50 1986

Hugh D. Huffaker, Jr. '48 1987

A. Warren James '43 1988

C. Houston Patterson, Jr. '43 1988

Gordon L. Smith, Jr. '43 1989

Fred W. Lazenby '50 1990

R. B. Davenport III '46 1991

Warren S. Gardner, Jr. '42 1992

Thomas A. Fanjoy '50 1993

Dan S. Blalock, Jr. '49 1994

Charles B. Lebovitz '55 1995

Spencer J. McCallie III '55 1995

James B. Williams '51 1996

Alan T. Dickson '49 1997

Edward G. Michaels III '60 1997

J. Hal Daughdrill III '73 1998

Fletcher Bright '49 1999

James W. Lail '45 2000

Edward Y. Chapin III '40 2001

Howard I. Levine '56 2003

David A. Stonecipher '59 2004

Honor Roll

McCallie School Teaching Faculty 1905 - 2005

With 20 years or more of service to McCallie

R. Kemmer Anderson 1977 - . . . . .28 Years
English

Ronald R. Ashlock 1971 - 1994 . . . . .23 Years
8th Grade French/ Social Studies/Director of Technology

Curtis F. Baggett '65 1972 - . . . . .33 Years
Mechanical Drawing/Physical Science/Environmental
Studies/Director of Admissions/Director of Development

Robert Hamilton Bailey 1970 - 1995 . . . . .26 Years
Chairman History Department/American History
Survey/Civil War & Reconstruction

Stephen L. Bartlett 1971 - . . . . .34 Years
History/Trainer/ Assistant Director of College Guidance

Dr. James Lewis Bibb 1913 - 1952 . . . . .40 Years
Hygiene/Physiology/Botany

Robert S. Bires 1983 - . . . . .22 Years
AP English/American Studies

Thomas S. Boyd 1974 - . . . . .31 Years
Chairman Science Department/AP Chemistry/Honors
Chemistry

William G. Boyd '65 1981 - 2002 . . . . .21 Years
7th Grade English

Grady S. Burgner 1981 - . . . . .24 Years
History

Arthur Lee Burns '20 1925 - 1972 . . . . .47 Years
Language Department Chairman/Associate Headmaster
1952-64/Dean of Students

William L. Cherry 1970 - . . . . .35 Years
Mathematics/Director of Athletics

Lewis F. Cisto 1985 - . . . . .20 Years
Music Department Chairman

Kenneth D. Cochrane 1969 – 1987, 1995 - . . . . .29 Years
Music Director 1968-1987/Director of Handbells 1995-

Gordon Connell 1980 - . . . . .25 Years
8th Grade Science

Melvin D. Cooper 1975 - . . . . .30 Years
Photography/Director of Development/VP for Planning &
Board Relations

John William Day 1953 - 1987 . . . . .34 Years
7th-Grade History/Junior School Principal

Col. Herbert Pritchard Dunlap 1925 - 1972 . . . . .47 Years
English II/Associate Headmaster 1952-55/Commandant

L. Harold Echart 1955 - 1988 .33 Years
Latin I/Economics/Social Studies/Modern History/
Summer School Principal

William C. Eiselstein 1967 - . . . . .38 Years
Pre-Calculus/AP Calculus I/Director Summer Programs

William Hugh Eskridge 1961 - 1989 . . . . .28 Years
8th Grade English

Terry N. Evans 1976 - . . . . .29 Years
7th Grade Science

C. Steven George 1971 - . . . . .34 Years
AP/9th-grade English/Director of College Guidance

Al L. Garth 1955 - 1981 . . . . .26 Years
Algebra I & II/Bible/Ancient History

David L. Hall 1983 - . . . . .22 Years
Bible Department Chairman

Hewitt E. Hubbert 1957 - 1977 . . . . .20 Years
Physics/Chemistry/Physical Science/Driver Education

Karen Hulvey 1985 - . . . . .20 Years
Keyboarding/Word Processing/Visual Basic

William O.E.A. Humphreys 1953 - 1991 . . . . .38 Years
Latin Department Chairman

A. Warren James '43 1952 - 1990 . . . . .38 Years
English/Shakespeare/Associate Headmaster 1978-1990

William L. Jamieson 1981 - . . . . .24 Years
English/Principal of Junior School

Marilyn A. Landis 1972 - . . . . .33 Years
Counselor/Human Development

Dr. Cleve Latham 1974 - . . . . .31 Years
Director of College Guidance/AP English/English

Chester LeSourd '72 1979 - . . . . .26 Years
English Department Chairman

Franklin E. Lewis '53 1966 - 2000 . . . . .34 Years
Computer Science/Chemistry/Dean of Faculty

Edwin C. Lundien 1951 - 1983 . . . . .32 Years
Biology

Thomas R. Makepeace '71 1976 - . . . . .29 Years
Mathematics Department Chairman

Mary K. May 1983 - . . . . .22 Years
Chemistry

Guy Simmons Mayberry 1943 - 1978 . . . . .35 Years
Military Science

Helen Maywhort 1959 - 1983 .24 Years
Librarian

John W. McCall '61 1969 - . . . . .36 Years
Spanish

Dr. James Park McCallie 1905 - 1971 . . . . .67 Years
Co-Founder/Co-Headmaster 1905-45/Headmaster 1945-49/
Mathematics/Bible

Dr. Robert Lewis McCallie '29 1933 - 1965 . . . . .32 Years
English/Co-Associate Headmaster 1946-49/
Co-Headmaster 1949-65

Prof. Spencer Jarnagin McCallie 1905 - 1949 .... 44 Years
Co-Founder/Co-Headmaster 1905-45/History/Bible

Mrs. Spencer J. McCallie 1922 - 1959 .... 38 Years
Librarian

Dr. Spencer Jarnagin McCallie Jr. '28 1932 - 1974 ... 43 Years
Mathematics/History/Bible/Co-Associate Headmaster
1946-49/Co-Headmaster 1949-65/Headmaster 1965-74

Spencer J. McCallie III '55 1963 -1999 .... 37 Years
Chairman of English Department/Director of Admission/
Headmaster 1974-99

Charles W. McDowell 1935 - 1967 .... 32 Years
Algebra/Trainer

Chalmers Moore Stirling McIlwaine '21 1925 – 1974 49 Years
Mathematics Department Chairman/Associate Headmaster
1952-64/Director of Alumni Affairs

Patrick D. McKinsey 1952 - 1988 .... 36 Years
Mathematics/Geometry/Psychology

Miles F. McNiff III 1961 - .... 44 Years
English/Director of Academics

Lance A. Nickel 1974 - .... 31 Years
Alumni Chair of Mathematics/Algebra II/AP Calculus

Dee Parker 1974 - 2003 .... 29 Years
Spanish

John T. Pataky '49 1957 - .... 48 Years
Mathematics

C. Houston Patterson Jr. '43 1948 - 1990 .... 42 Years
Geometry/Mathematics IV/Calculus/Associate Headmaster
1978-90

Pete Potter 1973 - 1994 .... 21 Years
Biology

William Wallace Purdy 1925 - 1956 .... 31 Years
Associate Headmaster 1952-56/Chemistry & Physics
Departments Chairman/Spanish/Music

Beth Reardon 1983 - .... 22 Years
Upper School Librarian

Z. Wayne Reynolds '65 1970 - .... 35 Years
Mathematics/Director of Testing

William A. Royer 1972 - .... 33 Years
French/Modern Language Department Chairman

Dr. Richard Lee Sager 1924 - 1944 .... 20 Years
Mathematics Department Chairman

Elliott Tourrett Schmidt, Sr. 1947 - 1987 .... 40 Years
History Department Chairman/Speech

Kenneth A Sholl 1983 - .... 22 Years
Mathematics Department Chairman/Head of the
Upper School

Richard I. Smith 1955 - 1985 .... 30 Years
Bible Department Chairman/Old & New Testament

Rev. W. Edward Snodgrass III '73 1985 - .... 21 Years
Joseph Glenn Sherrill Chair of Bible Chairholder

Col. David Monroe Spencer 1945 - 1972 .... 27 Years
Ancient History/ Economics

John Sharp Strang 1949 - 2003 .... 54 Years
7th Grade Bible

Dr. Richard A. Swanson 1977 - .... 28 Years
World History II/AP European History

Lewis Russell Tate '29 1940 - 1976 .... 36 Years
7th Grade English/Junior School Principal

William Anderson Venable 1920 - 1941 .... 21 Years
Latin

David R. Vining 1984 - .... 21 Years
7th-Grade Math

Pierre Wagner 1960 - 1989 .... 29 Years
French/German

Mary Louise Batey Walker 1939 - 1974 .... 35 Years
Latin/Assistant Librarian

Thomas Francis Walker '25 1943 - 1974 .... 31 Years
Spanish/French

John R. Wieczorek 1984 - .... 21 Years
Mathematics

Dr. Thomas Edward Peck Woods 1921 - 1948 .... 27 Years
Bible/English/Latin/Greek/Associate Headmaster 1921-45

Honor Roll

---◆---

McCallie School alumni who have died in military service

Name	Died	Conflict
CAPT William Forman Abernethy '57	7/21/67	Vietnam War
LT David Anderson Allen '34	3/19/45	World War II
2LT Michael Morrison Allison, Jr. '28	11/28/44	World War II
1LT Walter Moore Armistead '40	12/19/53	Korean War
1LT Frank Holmes Atlee '12	5/9/18	World War I
TSGT James Arthur Bacon, Jr. '42	11/10/44	World War II
SGT Ralph T. Bass '42	Unknown	World War II
LTC Charles Henry Mayhew Beatty '20	2/4/48	Peace Keeping
CAPT William Wiley Bird '36	7/29/46	Peace Keeping
1LT Henry McCoy Blanchard II '40	8/25/44	World War II
PFC Thomas Ruffin Bledsoe '37	11/30/42	World War II
LTC William Barringer Boyd '46	10/19/67	Vietnam War
PhM3/C Alfred Joseph Brandon, Jr. '27	9/26/45	World War II
2LT George Thomas Bright '43	6/14/45	World War II
PVT Nall Bright '23	11/13/44	World War II
MAJ John Wesley Browne, Jr. '35	4/2/57	Vietnam War
PVT John Walter Burton, Jr. '43	10/13/44	World War II
CAPT William Arthur Chenoweth, Jr. '34	7/29/43	World War II
LT Charles William Loring Clark '13	1918	World War I
LT William Gifford Clegg '41	12/5/44	World War II
LT Fabius Monroe Clements, Jr. '37	2/2/43	World War II
1LT Harry H. Cohn '38	6/11/44	World War II
1LT John Miles Corbett '43	12/15/52	Korean War
2LT Ruford Patterson Covington '42	6/12/45	World War II
SP4 Robert Barry Crosby '64	3/1/70	Vietnam War
LT Paul Winder Curtis, Jr. '31	12/21/44	World War II
LTJG Richard Clifton DeArmond, Jr. '60	7/13/66	Vietnam War
Gordon Dewees '19	1918	World War I
PVT George H. Dunlap IV '28	8/17/44	World War II
1SGT William Fitts Eldridge '34	3/2/45	World War II
1LT John Andrew Feuchtenberger '39	10/23/45	World War II
1LT Edwin Screven Frierson '42	11/21/44	World War II
Rhey P. Frierson '10	1918	World War I
CAPT Fred Weihl Fritts '10	10/9/18	World War I
PVT Lauren Allen Gates, Jr. '42	1/13/45	World War II
1LT James D. Gilbert '39	6/22/45	World War II
PFC John Turner Graves '43	2/21/45	World War II
1LT Clifford Barker Grayson '12	7/19/18	World War I
MAJ John Robert Hagan '63	5/6/69	Vietnam War
ENS Lemuel Woodward Harrison '42	10/27/44	World War II
2LT William Henry Harrison, Jr. '39	3/28/44	World War II
PFC James Perry Hartness, Jr. '43	7/22/45	World War II
S1/C William Peet Hemphill, Jr. '31	2/2/46	Peace Keeping
SGT Thomas Winchester Hendrick '43	1/8/45	World War II
LT Nelson Page Hill, Jr. '33	7/30/45	World War II
LT John McCormick Hodges III '78	2/27/93	Peace Keeping
2LT Spencer Hewitt Jarnagin '45	9/21/50	Korean War
CAPT Richard Henry Johnson '39	4/3/45	World War II
2LT Richard Sandusky Johnson, Jr. '62	3/26/67	Vietnam War
LT O. H. Perry Kenney '12	12/9/43	World War II
2LT William Robb Kimbro '47	12/12/50	Korean War
LT John McDowell King '41	5/4/44	World War II
1LT Walter Craig Lansford, Jr. '35	3/3/44	World War II
CDR Thomas Calloway Latimore '11	8/1941	World War II
SGT Eugene Robinson Matthews '32	3/11/45	World War II
SGT Frank Dean May '41	4/6/45	World War II
LT Charles Asbery McKinney '37	1943	World War II
MAJ William Thomas McPhail '57	5/22/68	Vietnam War
LT Harvey Wilson Moore, Jr. '33	6/19/43	World War II
CPL Charles Harwood Moorman '43	8/7/44	World War II
PFC Morris Belknap Moorman '43	7/18/44	World War II
PVT Raymond W. Mullins '35	6/27/44	World War II
ENS Robert Goree Nelson, Jr. '39	9/12/45	World War II
PFC David Montgomery Nicoll '50	5/22/51	Korean War
AMN Scott Roberts Oliver '80	8/23/83	Peace Keeping
S3/C Frank Harwood Pennybacker '41	5/8/42	World War II
1LT Billy Charles Perry, Jr. '79	3/20/90	Peace Keeping
Thomas Merritt Pittman, Jr. '37	5/27/42	World War II
A2/C Earl Wilbur Radlein, Jr. '50	7/29/53	Korean War
ENS Robert Eugene Ridenhour III '41	8/27/45	World War II
ENS George Scarboro Roberts '56	12/28/62	Vietnam War
PFC Ben Bob Ross '44	11/22/44	World War II
2LT Frank Thatcher Saunders, Jr. '39	1/11/44	World War II
1LT Frederick A. Schlemmer '40	7/11/44	World War II
SSGT John Montgomery Schneider, Jr. '42	11/11/44	World War II
1LT William David Settlemire '62	2/9/66	Vietnam War
1LT Marshall McLaney Shepherd '36	10/8/43	World War II
1LT Joseph Glenn Simpson '38	10/29/42	World War II
PFC John Graham Sims '39	12/16/44	World War II
2LT Robert Emerson Smitherman '40	2/3/45	World War II
LT Kenneth Steward, Jr. '36	4/4/43	World War II
LTJG Garner P. Strickland, Jr. '41	6/13/49	Peace Keeping
LT Paul Andrew Swank '39	8/17/44	World War II
PFC Edward Gilbert Taliaferro '43	12/9/44	World War II
2LT John Ashley Templeton '63	7/18/68	Vietnam War
Benjamin Bryant Todd, Jr. '37	1942	World War II
CAPT Charles Hector Triplett III '36	6/15/44	World War II
2LT Fred C. Wallace, Jr. '40	7/19/44	World War II
SSGT William Durham West, Jr. '43	3/20/45	World War II
LT William Henry Wilson III '36	8/22/43	World War II
PVT Charles Sumpter Wylie '43	12/7/44	World War II
2LT Louis Gray Young '42	3/30/45	World War II

McCallie School Alumni Achievement Award Recipients

1984
James Clifford Crawford, Jr. '44
Charles Edward Bugg '59
Emerson Barney Robinson, Jr. '59

1985
Robert Thomas Amos, Jr. '40
James Walter Lail '45
Richard Barry McCubbin '45
Paul Kruesi Brock '50
William Buchanan Dunavant, Jr. '50
Fred Wiehl Lazenby '50
Rev. Fred Taylor II '50
Charles Baras Lebovitz '55

1986
Judge John Pierre Hill '26
Esley Offit Anderson, Jr. '31
Ernest Koella, Jr. '36
Dr. William Henry Muller, Jr. '36
Dr. Thomas Sampson Royster, Jr. '36
Joseph Howard Davenport, Jr. '41
Dr. Robert Day McAmis '41
James Lander Morgan '41
Dr. Herschell Hood Boyd '46
Rodolph Blevins Davenport III '46
Dr. Robin Martin Rudoff '51
James Bryan Williams '51
Hon. Lewis Homer Conner, Jr. '56
Charles George Mills '56
Rodolph Gordon Sherrill '56
Henry Belden Aldridge, Ph.D. '61
Dr. Archer Wortman Bishop, Jr. '61
James Robert Martin '61
John Leachman Oliver, Jr. '61
James Creekmore Wann, Jr. '66

1987
Edward Balloff '37
Sloan Young Bashinsky '37
George Stephenson Hazard '37
Dr. John Chalmers Vinson '37
Alexander White Wells '37
James Fielder Cook '42
James Forest Smith, Jr. '47
Dr. Edward Castello Loughlin, Jr. '52

Dr. Louis Loraine Carter, Jr. '57
Dr. James Allen Vann III '57
John Hoyle Rymer '62
Eugene Harrison Schimpf III '67
CAPT Thomas Allen Gardner, Jr.,
    USN '72

1988
Richard Acree Brock '33
COL Richard Sandusky Johnson '33
LaFayette Turner Prigmore, Jr. '38
Judge Lapsley Walker Hamblen, Jr. '43
Dr. Thomas E. Whitesides, Jr. '48
Robert Faucette Huffaker '53
Gov. Carroll Ashmore Campbell, Jr. '58
David Jarvis Cocke '63
David Milton Muhlendorf '68
Harvey Hill Carrow, Jr. '73

1989
Lewis Russell Tate '29
John Austin Tate, Jr. '34
Dr. Edwin Brabson Anderson '39
John Montgomery Belk '39
Dr. William Bryce Hunt, Jr. '44
George Henry Cornelson IV '49
Dr. Louis Henderson Zbinden, Jr. '54
Dr. Leland Madison Park '59
Dr. Edward Lamar Baker, Jr. '64
Ernest Robert Cotter III '69

1990
Dr. Thomas McCallie Divine '20
George Marvin Lewis, Jr. '35
Chester Oliver Stephens, Jr. '40
Dr. Joseph Elliott Blaydes, Jr. '45
John Lutz III '50
Spencer Jarnagin McCallie III '55
Dr. John Daniel Gray Rather V '55
Charles Henry Battle, Jr. '60
Edward Griffin Michaels III '60
Joseph Patrick Congleton '65
Dr. Daniel Frederick Chambliss '70
John Douglas Snodgrass '75

1991
Dr. Ebenezer Alexander, Jr. '31
James Henry Millis, Sr. '41
William Loomis Burns, Jr. '46
Frank McClelland Mitchener, Jr. '51
James Lloyd Rogers III '56
Dr. Ronald Baker Cox '61
Edward Jackson Hardin '61
Sanford Brooks Prater '66
Dr. Arthur Palfrey Bode, Ph.D. '71
Dr. Tarek Makansi '76

1992
Dr. James Hubert Taliaferro, Jr. '42
James Columbus Talley II '42
Samuel Brinson Hollis '47
Samuel Henegar Campbell III '52
Charles Randolph Wedding '52
James Case Richards '77

1993
Robert Mercer Vance '33
Sen. Douglas Selph Henry, Jr. '43
Dr. William Jackson Payne, Sr. '43
Frank Williams McDonald '48
Norman Clark Schlemmer '48
Charles Emile Kohlhase, Jr. '53
Thomas Ferran Frist '63
Marshall Fletcher McCallie '63
Clay Redman Caroland III '73
Dr. Rance Cleaveland '78

1994
William McElwee Miller, Jr. '44
Dr. Woodruff Asbury Banks, Jr. '49
Daniel Simeon Blalock, Jr. '49
Robert Edward Helms '59
David Allen Stonecipher '59
Paul Campbell III '64
Robert Kirk Walker, Jr., Ph.D. '69

1995
Donald Richard Jones II '45
George Franklin Walker '45
Henry Louis Diamond, Jr. '50
John Nevius Lukens, Jr. '50

Honor Roll

Dr. Ned Carroll Watts, Jr. '55
Dr. Frank Acree Brock '60
Dr. Hugh Agnew Gamble II '65
Meredith Baird Allen '70
Stephen Charles Schram '75
Samuel Albert Sims '80

1996

Sen. William Ward Crutchfield '46
Robert Thomas Jones, M.D. '46
Dr. Charles Blanton Cousar '51
James Park McCallie II '56
CDR Charles Mills Wood III '61
Sergio Paiz '66
Dr. Edward Norwood Robinson, Jr. '71
The Honorable Zachary Paul Wamp '76

1997

Thomas Milburn Belk '42
Henry Clifton Humphreys, Jr. '47
Dr. Richard B. Patterson '47
Thomas Wilton Wade, Jr. '52
Timothy Brian Robertson '72
Giovanni Alberto Agnelli III '82
Jon Ellis Meacham '87

1998

COL (Ret.) Jack P. Lansford, USA '38
Dr. Charles Robert Clark '48
Daniel Brown Rather '53
Franklin Scanlon McCallie '58
Barry Wayne Parker '63
Thomas Walter Dickson '73
Robert Carter Divine '78

1999

Frank Spain Dennis, Jr. '39
Edwin Lee Jones, Jr. '39
Richard Scott Morris '49
The Rev. Dr. Albert Mitchell
    Pennybacker '49
CAPT George Willis Lundy, Jr. '59
Halbert Grant Law, Jr. '64
William Neel Carpenter '69
Hon. Carl Horn, III '69
Graeme McGregor Keith, Jr. '74
John Tally Johnston III '79
Daniel Timothy Castor '84

2000

William Bonner McCarty, Jr. '40
William Murphy Marine, M.D.,
    M.P.H. '50
Dr. Dave McAlister Davis '55
Harry Whitney Durand III '60
Curtis Franklin Baggett '65
Dr. Robert Bruce Betz '70
Timothy Allen Stump '75
Joseph Edward Petty '80

2001

Irwin Isaac Belk '41
Samuel Francis Fowler, Jr. '46
Dr. Robert Ernest Steel, Jr. '46
Edward McMurray Fisher '51
Howard Ivan Levine '56
Hon. William Bilbo Mitchell Carter '61
John Wells McCravey, M.D. '66
Dr. Charles Baker Felts III '71
Robert Campbell Taylor, Jr. '76

2002

Dr. John Clement Whitcomb, Jr. '42
Dr. Will Walker Ward, Jr. '47
Jay Lewis Levine '52
Joseph William Camp, Jr. '57
Hugh Jacob Moore, Jr. '62
James Edward Glasser '67
William Henry Chapin '72
Dr. John Robert Roberts '77
Dr. John Clifton Wellons III '87

2003

Samuel Heron Carter, Jr. '43
Dr. John Thomas Christian '53
John D. McConnell, Jr. '58
Paul Edwin Good, Jr. '63
Dr. Clifford Walter Shults '68
John A. Fogarty, Jr. '73
Mark Huebner Oldham '78
John Anderson Bobo, Jr. '83
Wilmer Hastings Mills '88

2004

Hon. William Robert Baker '49
John Robert Johnson '54
Rev. George Edgar Milner, Jr. '54
William Jeremiah Branstrom III '59
RADM Robert Cameron Crates, SC,
    USNR (Ret.) '59
Dr. Maurice Scaggs Rawlings '69
R. Timothy Culvahouse '74
Stephen David Lebovitz '79
Douglas Randolph Wedding '79
Joseph Parnell Ferguson '84

Alma Mater

McCallie, dear McCallie School
Thy loyal sons are we;
Strong in thy strength
We'll ever stand
And true we'll always be.
In thee we place
Our fondest trust,
For thee our prayers shall rise;
Oh, Alma Mater,
Hail, all hail!
We lift our song to thee.
Oh, Alma Mater,
Hail, all hail!
We lift our song to thee.

Arthur L. Burns '20